SHEPHERD, SAILOR AND SURVIVOR

THE LIFE AND LETTERS OF

JAMES HYSLOP, R.N.

1764 – 1853

By his great-great-great-grand-niece

Dorothy Hyslop Booth

Published in 2010 by
D. H. Booth & E. D. Booth
3 Raasay Road
Inverness IV2 3LR
Scotland

ISBN 978-0-9542635-1-5

Printed and bound by ForTheRightReasons Community Print

This book is dedicated to my mother

Hilda McVittie Cooper

who had given me so much information

in family stories about James Hyslop

and had left written notes on many of the

relatives mentioned in his letters.

Acknowledgments

I wish to record my thanks to the many people who have helped me with my research and given suggestions as to where to make further enquiries.

The Staff of Inter-Library Loans, Library Support Unit, Inverness; H E Jones, Research, Knowledge and Academic Services Department, National Archives, Kew; Stephen Potter, Southwark Local History Library; Peter Craven, Pastoral Department, Diocese of Southwark; Staff at the Reference Library, Inverness; Sue Weir, Medical History Tours, London; Richard Adams; Peter Clark; David M Fowler; Andrew Fraser; Anne Gillies; Dorothy Hadley; Tony Little; Brian Meringo; Véronique Miller; Robina Morris; Bob and Anna Newman; Gordon and Mollie Rowe; Ellen Squires; Doreen and Ian Thomson; Edith van Driel; Alan Wilkinson; Also professional researchers Michael Gandy; Peter Houghton; Andy Plant.

Most especially I want to express my gratitude to my sons. Ewan has scanned onto computer all the photographs, family trees, James's letters to the Minister of War and the letter from Colonel Charles W. Pasley. Malcolm helped with the design of the cover, and has provided continued help and encouragement including chaperoning me to various research centres in a busy and confusing city.

CONTENTS

ILLUSTRATIONS

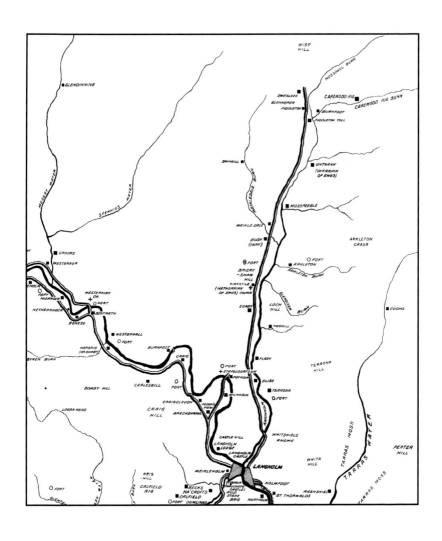

Upper Eskdale and Ewesdale

8

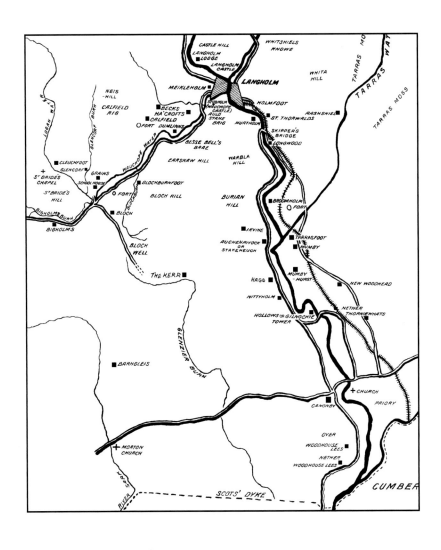

Lower Eskdale and Wauchopedale

9

PREFACE

My late husband, Alan, was born in Canada of a Canadian father and a Scottish mother but had lived in Scotland since 1930. I had never met anyone who knew less about his family history! In 1980 we visited his Uncle and Aunt in Winnipeg and I asked about his Canadian ancestors who had emigrated from Britain. Aunt Ann remembered that there was a hymn book down in the basement which had belonged to great-grandmother Elizabeth Moore. On the fly leaf was her name and "Saleby, 1847". We had no idea where that was but found it to be a hamlet in Lincolnshire next to Maltby-le-Marsh. So we joined the Lincolnshire Family History Society.

When Alan died in 1997 I had really finished all possible research into the Moore family but never cancelled my membership of the society and this was fortuitous. In 1999 on June 5 my journal from the society arrived and there I found an article by Michael Read about his great-great-grandfather Captain George Read who had been a prisoner at Verdun. His ship had been captured by the French in 1803. In his possession he had a log book belonging to midshipman, Samuel Robinson, who had been shipwrecked on the Frigate *HMS Shannon*. The name of the ship was familiar and I was almost certain that it was the ship on which Uncle James had been wrecked and taken prisoner. Sure enough it was. I immediately wrote to the Editor* and sent a copy of my letter to Michael Read explaining my interest in the *Shannon*. Michael telephoned me as soon as he had received my letter and we had a long talk about our research interests.

In February 2002 I had another call from Michael to say that he was planning to take a party of his relatives to Verdun by bus sometime in 2003, two hundred years after our ancestors had been shipwrecked. Would I like to join the group? Well of course I would!

At that time I had not done any research into James's life as I had been working on producing an updated edition of *Langholm As It Was* which was due to be published that June. So my research really began in the autumn of 2002. The work has been very intermittent due to illness and many other family commitments.

On Sunday 1st June 2003 at 6.30am I joined twenty-six Read descendants on the bus journey from Horncastle to Verdun where we arrived at 6pm. There we were joined by several others including Professor Peter Clark, historian and an authority on the history of prisoners during the Napoleonic wars.

The next day we had a guided tour of the old part of Verdun. When we arrived at the old and original gates at the entrance to the Citadel Peter suggested to the young official guide that he explained the history and importance of the fortress. The guide was both interested and astonished at his knowledge and thereafter Peter continued to be the guide of the tour. That evening Peter had organised some of us into producing a playlet where we read extracts from letters and contemporary accounts of life in Verdun 1803-1814. The guide was invited and other guests included the deputy mayor of Verdun and his wife.

I am greatly indebted to and wish to record my thanks to Michael for organising the trip and for his and his wife Sheena's hospitality. My thanks also go to Peter who gave us all so much information about Verdun.

The visit to Verdun had been so interesting that I decided to look into James's career in the navy which entailed many visits to the National Archives at Kew. My first visit was somewhat nerve wracking as a detailed knowledge of computers was required but all the staff were most helpful and sympathetic to a complete novice. All my research took far longer than I had anticipated because each new fact provided another point to investigate. I found that three days at a time were all I could cope with as by then my brain had reached saturation point. It is also quite physically tiring as many of the books I wanted to examine were so large and heavy that one had to visit the map room up another three flights of stairs. Then it was home to assimilate the information and write another chapter.

It has been fascinating work putting the background to each of James's letters and to me he has become alive. I think the most thrilling part of my visit to Verdun was to walk through the entrance

11

gate, La Porte Chausée, through which James must have walked many times.

The most difficult research has been the years after James retired and resulted in visits to various record offices in the north of England. There too the staff have always been most helpful. This has all been very time consuming but extremely rewarding.

This book is produced mainly for my family but I hope may be of interest to others.

CHAPTER 1

UNCLE JAMES

Uncles were thin on the ground in my childhood whereas Aunts were ten a penny. In the 1930's no child would have addressed an adult by a first name; it was always Mr. or Mrs. So-and-so, or in the case of family friends, Auntie, or very infrequently, Uncle.

I had numerous aunts. When I was about eight years old I became curious as to who they all were. I knew I had only two "proper" aunts, my father's sisters, so who were all these others? There was Auntie Jean, my grandfather's elder sister and Auntie Sarah, his younger sister and Aunt Mary who was addressed as Aunt even by my grandfather. Some of the aunts were cousins of my mother while others were just family friends. It was all very confusing to a child so my mother began to draw up the family tree in order to explain it all to me. This I found fascinating and my interest in genealogy and family history really stems from that time.

And then an Uncle was mentioned! This was exciting after all the Aunts. Furthermore this Uncle James had led an adventurous life. He had been to sea, travelled to faraway places, had been shipwrecked and captured by the French. He spent ten years as a prisoner of war at Verdun and his letters home survived in the family for more than a hundred years. Unfortunately the letters are no longer extant but during the late 1850's, they were copied into an exercise book by a grand-nephew. The cover of the book says "William Hyslop, Langholm, December 1855". William developed tuberculosis and died in 1859 aged twenty-two. According to his death certificate he had been ill for three years. Perhaps copying out the letters was occupational therapy for him. This book was in my grandfather Robert Hyslop's possession and I eventually inherited it from my mother.

James Hyslop was born on the 26th September 1764 at Old Irvine, in the Parish of Langholm, Dumfriesshire and was baptised on the 30th. He was the third son of Walter Hyslop, Tailor in Old Irvine, a farm township high up on the hillside about two miles south of Langholm. His mother was Elizabeth (Lizzie) Little, the sixth child and fifth daughter of Simon Little in Terrona in the Parish of Ewes.

James would be educated at Langholm Parish School which was noted for its high academic standards. At the end of the 17th century the Church of Scotland had ordered that all parish schools should receive financial support from the local landowners, thus enabling all children, regardless of their background, to have the chance of a good education. The Parish School in Langholm had, in the latter part of the 18th century, a particularly able teacher, John Telfer, whose appointment in 1771 is mentioned in the Langholm Presbytery Records.

Verbal family history relates that the sea had always held a fascination for James but his parents were askance at the very idea of him joining the Navy as a young boy, and he was too considerate of their feelings to run away to sea. They expected him to follow his father as a tailor but he knew that trade was not for him. He continued to live with his parents at Old Irvine and was employed as a shepherd.

The second half of the 18th century was a time of great expansion in overseas commerce and possessions, and great was the rivalry between British and French colonists and traders in India and North America. In 1756 war broke out between Britain and France, at the end of which Clive had defeated the French in India and Wolfe secured Quebec and French Canada for Britain. British victories were to a large extent due to the mastery of the oceans by the Royal Navy. Overseas trade could not be carried out without merchant ships but frequently these Merchantmen required the protection of the Navy. Men from greatly respected local families in Langholm — Paisleys, Malcolms and Littles — served in the Army, Navy and East India Company and many a thrilling and adventurous story must have filtered home. It was probably exciting accounts of Naval exploits and the lure of foreign lands which had fired James's childhood imagination. What better way to visit these places than a career at sea? His interest in people and fascination with new places, which he often described in great detail, is shown in many of his letters.

In James's early years rapid development was taking place in Langholm and the surrounding dales. The Heritable Jurisdictions Act of 1747 had released farmers from the tyranny of thirlage, which had placed them at the mercy of the miller and greatly hampered the natural evolution of agriculture. They now had freedom of choice as to where they took their grain to be milled. They were also relieved from their obligation to give so much free labour to their landlords and to his levy on their produce. A quicker and readier market was being found and the great Fairs, such as the Langholm Summer Fair, served as excellent markets for sheep and wool.

The enormous power of the House of Buccleuch had also been considerably curtailed by the Act of 1747. Henry, third Duke of Buccleuch, succeeded just at the time of the great revival of agriculture in Scotland. His knowledge and interest in agriculture was extensive. He had received the sum of £1,400 as compensation for the loss of his baronial rights and this money was spent largely on the development of his estate. In this he was ably assisted by his baron-bailie, Matthew Little.

One of the Duke's most important actions was the laying out of the New-Town of Langholm on the western side of the river Esk. The land for this was provided by the breaking up of the farm of Meikleholm. In order to expand the town to the other side of the river it was obviously necessary to have a bridge and the building of Langholm Bridge, by Robert (Robin) Hotson, began in 1775 and was completed in 1778. The cost was met by public subscription, liberally supported by the farmers in the neighbouring parishes of Westerkirk and Eskdalemuir, who were quick to see the business advantage it would give them. The building of about 140 houses in the New-Town began in 1778 and continued for the next 20 years. This not only provided better accommodation but gave much needed employment in the area.

15

Industries, too, were becoming established. The writer of the Statistical Account of 1793 notes that there were six manufacturers in checks, thread or stockings and forty-three weavers. There was also a paper mill employing twenty workers.

In March 1788 James's father died but James continued to live at Old Irvine with his mother. His brothers were all away from home. Simon, the eldest, was a merchant in Langholm. John served his apprenticeship with Robin Hotson, mason and builder, and continued to work for him. Walter, the youngest, was a joiner in Langholm. Soon however there would be a new interest to occupy Lizzie.

On June 30th her son John became the father of a daughter, Magdalen, or Maddy as she was called as a child. For the first few years of her life she was brought up by her grandmother and lived at Old Irvine, so James's concern for her welfare, expressed in many of his letters, is understandable. Maddy's mother was Elizabeth Reid. Did her mother die in childbirth or was Maddy born as a result of hand-fasting? No trace of this Elizabeth Reid can be found in the Old Parish Records so we shall never know.

Hand-fasting was a modified form of marriage and was performed at Handfasting Haugh situated, appropriately, where the waters of the Black Esk and White Esk unite. It was observed by the parties clasping hands in token of their mutual contract. The marriage existed for a year, on the expiry of which either person could annul it, in which case due care was taken to recognise the legitimacy of any offspring and the one opting out of the handfasting was responsible for the child's maintenance. If the parties were mutually agreeable to the union, or had failed to have it annulled within the required period, the marriage was made absolute. Hand-fasting was, of course, anathema to the Church and the entry in Langholm Old Parish Register records her baptism thus:

"1788 July. Magdalen, daughter natural to John Hyslop, Mason, late in Irvine, now in New Langholm, and Elizabeth Reid, daughter of David Reid, weaver in Milntown, the father now absolved, being sponsor. Born June 30 last."

The year 1794 was disastrous for all the farms in Eskdale. One of the most severe snow storms ever recorded at that time started on January 23rd. It became known as *The Gonial Blast*, so named because of the extraordinary number of sheep which perished. Gonial was the name applied to the mutton of sheep found dead and from which smoked mutton-hams were produced. The storm continued for several days, snow, rain and frost alternating in quick succession and in the Langholm area over 4000 sheep were either smothered, frozen or drowned. With few sheep remaining shepherds were in dire straits. Conditions became even more desperate when the autumn of 1794 saw the first of a succession of bad harvests and this was followed by a further severe winter. Many farmers and their families were at starvation level.

In April 1795 Lizzie died aged 69. Whether her death was the result of the recent harsh living conditions we shall never know. On the 6th August 1790 her son John had married his boss's daughter, Agnes (Nanny) Hotson. They had a son Walter aged 4 who later died when he was ten years old. Their first daughter had died aged two months and their second daughter had died in March 1795. Such was infant mortality. After her grandmother's death Maddy went to live with her father and his wife while James, free at last from family responsibilities, was able to fulfil his dreams of a career at sea.

CHAPTER 2

WHO'S WHO

In all his letters James is meticulous in sending greetings to his many relatives and friends. An explanantion as to who they all are is required. Most of his relatives have been located through family history research as have many of his friends and aquaintances; however there are a few who remain a mystery.

FAMILY

Simon HYSLOP, 1758-1834, James's eldest brother, was a merchant in Langholm. It was to him that James wrote his letters. In October 1804 James wishes to be remembered to the Goodwife so evidently Simon married but no record has been found. Simon's death is recorded on the same stone as his parents in Wauchope Kirkyard but no spouse recorded.

John HYSLOP, 1761-1809, was a mason and builder in Langholm. He served his apprenticeship with Robin Hotson, builder of Langholm Bridge. On 6th August 1790 he married Robin Hotson's eldest child, AGNES, 1767-1850, known in the family as Nanny, the diminutive of Agnes. They had eleven children of whom six survived to adulthood. John died as the result of an accident in 1809 leaving his wife to bring up Robert, Simon, William, Walter, James and John.

Walter HYSLOP, 1768-1824, the youngest, was a joiner. In the autumn of 1801 he went to work on a sugar plantation in Jamaica.

Magdalen HYSLOP, or Maddy, natural daughter of John Hyslop and Elizabeth Reid. In 1809 she married Robert SCOON, Mason in Langholm.

RELATIVES

Many of his relatives were tenant farmers and frequently James simply refers to them by the name of the farm.

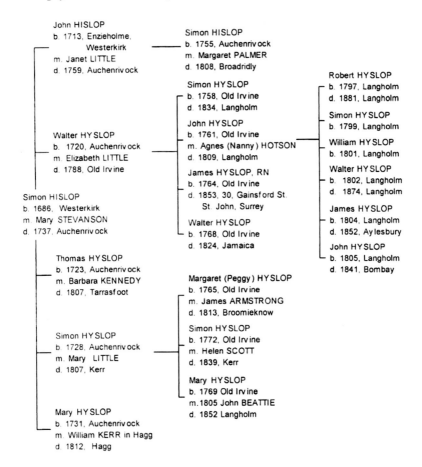

Family tree of Hyslop relatives.

AUCHENRIVOCK. Uncle Thomas HYSLOP, 1723-1807 was a younger brother of James's father. Born at Auchenrivock where he worked for many years he married Barbara Kennedy. He died in 1807 at Tarrasfoot where he was probably living with his daughter, Joan.

CROFTHEAD. (near Auchenrivock) Some of Thomas Hyslop's family.

THE KERR. Uncle Simon HYSLOP, 1728-1807, was another younger brother of James's father. He was born at Auchenrivock. He worked at first on the farm of Old Irvine before becoming a tenant farmer at The Kerr. He married Mary LITTLE, 1732-1819, younger sister of James's mother. Their children were all born at Old Irvine. Margaret, or Peggy, 1765-1813, married James ARMSTRONG, in Broomieknowe. Simon, 1772-1839, continued to farm at The Kerr and married Helen SCOTT. Mary, 1769-1852, married John BEATTIE.

HAGG. Aunt Mary HYSLOP, 1731-1812, was the youngest sister of James's father. She married William KERR tenant farmer in Hagg.

TERRONA. Uncle James LITTLE, 1741-99, was the youngest brother of James's mother. His two sons are mentioned occasionally in the letters. ARCHIBALD, 1774-1850, remained at home. He was a waster and generally regarded by the rest of the family as a disaster. SIMON, 1769-, was a Purser in the Royal Navy. He received his Warrant 24 November 1794 and was appointed to HMS Illustrious. In 1801 he was purser on HMS Sampson and that year transfers to HMS Donegal. In 1818 he is on HMS Ramillies.`

CAREWOODRIG (sometimes Carrickrig or Carretrig) a farm in Ewesdale near Unthank. Aunt Janet LITTLE, 1734-1815 sister of James's mother, married William MURRAY. Their sons were Simon who died in 1805 aged 28 and Thomas who died in 1813 aged 34. Their daughter Violet married Adam Paterson. She died in 1855 aged 80. They are all buried in Ewes Kirkyard but Janet is called Jane on the gravestone, whereas at baptism she is Janet. The missing letter "t" may be due to weathering of the stone.

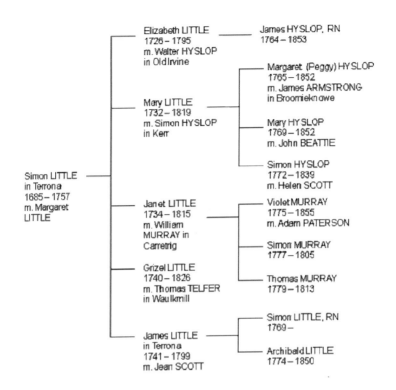

Family tree of Little relatives.

MIDDLEBYHILL. Janet HYSLOP, sister of James's grandfather Simon, was married on the 15th June 1713 in the parish of Westerkirk to James BEATTIE farmer in the parish of Middleby.

THOMAS TELFER, lived at Waulkmill, Westerkirk and married Grizel LITTLE, 1740-1826, sister of James's mother. He died in 1802, aged 65 and is buried at Westerkirk. After his death Grizel went to live with her sister, Mary, at the Kerr until she died there aged 86. She is buried at Westerkirk with her husband.

JAMES STOTHART, with whom James lodged temporarily before joining the Royal Navy, married Jane SCOTT. Her sister Helen was married to James's cousin Simon Hyslop in Kerr. Kinship, was very important at that time and most families, if the need were to arise, would help a relative however remotely connected.

SIR JAMES LITTLE, 1761-1829, was the second son of Matthew Little, baron-bailie of Langholm, and Helen Pasley. He was a wine merchant in Tenerife.

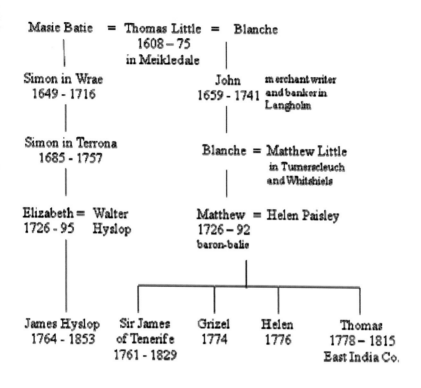

Relationship of James Hyslop and Sir James Little.

For his outstanding services rendered during a yellow fever epidemic, he was made a Knight of the Most Illustrious Spanish Order of Charles the Third, Sacred to Virtue and Merit. As he could not use this title in Britain some of his friends prevailed upon King George III to award him a British Knighthood. He was very distantly related to James, both being great-great-grandsons of Thomas Little, 1608-75, Laird in Meikledale.

Thomas Little, his son Simon in Wrae and grandson Simon in Terrona are all buried in Ewes Kirkyard; their names are on the gravestone so James's Little lineage is known. According to the

Little pedigree drawn up by Bluemantle in 1811 John Little, merchant, writer and banker in Langholm was another son of Thomas Little. This would mean that James would be distantly related to James Little in Tenerife, Thomas in Bombay and the two Misses Little, Grizel and Helen. In his letters he certainly appears to be on friendly terms with them all. I am indebted to Edith van Driel, Australia, and Tony Little, New Zealand; they found Thomas Little's second wife and gave me the information which has allowed me to produce the Little Tree shown on the previous page. My thanks to them both.

FRIENDS AND AQUAINTANCES

In order of appearance, but unfortunately there are a few who cannot be identified.

ADMIRAL SIR THOMAS PASLEY, born in Westerkirk near Langholm was the fifth son of James Paisley of Craig and his wife Magdalen Elliot. He entered the Royal Navy and rose to the rank of Rear-Admiral of the Red. In this position he was on the *Bellerophon* and fought under Admiral Howe's command at the naval battle of the "Glorious First of June" in 1794 when the Royal Navy defeated the French. In this action he had a leg shot off and lost an eye. As a token of respect to Viscount Horatio Nelson, who lost an eye in the same year, he dropped the letter "I" from his surname. For his distinguished service he was created Baronet of G.B. and given a pension of £1000 a year and the post of Commander-in-Chief at Plymouth.

THE MISS LITTLES were Grizel and Helen daughters of Matthew Little, baron-bailie, and his wife Helen Pasley, sister of Admiral Pasley.

MRS. MALCOLM was Margaret (or Peggy) Pasley, another younger sister of the Admiral. She married George Malcolm son of the Rev. Robert Malcolm, minister of Ewes Parish.

MR. JAMIESON. Thomas Jamieson was a ship and insurance broker at 17 London Street, Paddington, London.

ROBERT (Robin) HOTSON, 1831-1813, mason and builder, father of James's sister-in-law Nanny. According to the Langholm Old Parish Records he was buried on 6th January 1813. On his gravestone his year of death is given incorrectly as 1818; monumental inscriptions are not always correct and should be checked with other sources if possible.

GENERAL SIR CHARLES PASLEY. He was born in January 1781, son of Charles Pasley. During his early childhood he was looked after by Elizabeth Little, James's mother. This information is contained in a letter dated October 1824, still extant, which Charles wrote to Elizabeth's daughter-in-law, Agnes Hyslop. James, in his letter dated November 1798, asks what Charles is doing now. In 1796 Charles had entered the Royal Academy at Woolwich, and in 1797 received a commission in the royal artillery. In 1798 he transferred to the royal engineers. Later he was director of military engineering instruction at Chatham.

MAJOR THOMAS LITTLE, 1777-1815, fifth son of Matthew Little and Helen Paisley, had a distinguished career in the East India Service. In September 1803 he was Aide de Camp to General Wellesley at the battle of Assaye. In 1809 he had command of the Guard of Honour to Sir John Malcolm, Ambassador to Persia.

JOHN PASLEY, elder brother of Admiral Pasley, lived at 66 Gower Street, London. He was a merchant with the East India Company.

CHARLES PASLEY, younger brother of Admiral Pasley, was a Merchant and Wine Agent in Lisbon. In 1802 his address is 21, Thavies-inn, Holborn.

MISS MALCOLM was probably Agnes, 1763-1836, second daughter of George Malcolm and Peggy Paisley The eldest daughter, Magdalen, had died in 1779 at the age of 17.

MR. BELL was Joseph the elder brother of John Bell, ship's surgeon. Joseph was baptised in the parish of Kirkoswald, near Penrith, on 16 February 1770. He appears to have been based in London. On 18th April 1801 he married Amey Kimber at St. Saviour's Church in Southwark. St. Saviour's became Southwark Cathedral in 1905.

CAPTAIN PULTENEY MALCOLM, born in 1768, third son of George Malcolm and Peggy Pasley, entered the Royal Navy and served under his uncle Admiral Sir Thomas.

CAPTAIN CHARLES MALCOLM, born in 1782, tenth and youngest son of George Malcolm. He entered Naval Service and served at first under his brother Pulteney.

The REV. THOMAS MARTIN, minister at Langholm Parish Kirk 1791 to 1812. He wrote the history of the parish for the 1793 Statistical Account.

The REV. JOHN JARDINE was the first minister appointed in 1789 to the Secession Kirk which became the North United Presbyterian Kirk; he remained there until his death in 1820.

DR. JAMES MOFFAT, born 1767, had his medical practice in Langholm. According to his gravestone in Westerkirk he was the son of James Moffat of Midknock and Mary Armstrong. James mentions him in many of his letters and they were obviously good friends.

COL. MURRAY is Matthew Murray who had been in Bombay with the East India Company. He died in Langholm on 6th June 1811, aged 62, and is buried in Wauchope Kirkyard.

DR. DOUGLAS. The Militia List compiled in 1802 mentions a Thomas Douglas, surgeon in Langholm.

JOHN HOTSON, 1770-1848, eldest son of Robert, was a thread manufacturer in New Langholm. He married Isabella Anderson. In 1802 he is on the Militia List.

JAMES CARRUTHERS restarted with his brother John the cotton manufactory in 1794 at Meikleholm Mill. Originally founded in 1789, it had to close in 1793 due to nation-wide financial difficulties.

ALEXANDER HOTSON, 1777-1857, son of Robert, was a mason and builder in Langholm. He married Grizel Nicol. Several of his children emigrated to Canada.

MRS. MOFFAT. Born Margaret Borthwick in 1733, daughter of William Borthwick, tenant in Howpasley. She married James Moffat, born in Howpasley in 1721 and later tenant in Garwald who died in 1779. She died in July 1806 according to the gravestone in

Watcarrick Kirkyard. Her son William married Jane Grieve. Her daughter, Margaret married the REV. DR. BROWN, minister at Eskdalemuir and writer of the 1793 Statistical Account for that parish.

I.HOPE is ISOBEL, 1769-1851, daughter of John Hope, weaver in Langholm and his wife Barbara Murray.

NATHAN LINTON, 1770-1833, merchant in Langholm, was the son of John Linton and Margaret Little.

MR. CORRIE. There is a John Corrie listed in several trade directories from 1790, as a Timber Merchant in Vauxhall. It is impossible to know if he is the person James mentions in so many letters.

MR. WILLIAM MOFFAT resided at 32 Queen's Square, Bloomsbury, merchant and tea-broker in Watling Street

SIMON IRVING was a merchant in London. Born in 1769, son of Janetus Irving, 1741-1815, baker, and his wife Helen, 1737-97, daughter of Simon Little in Nittyholm.

MR. ARMSTRONG, Wrae, is William, tenant farmer, who died in 1811, buried in Stapelgortoun Kirkyard. His son Archibald died in 1810.

CHAPTER 3

THE FIRST VOYAGE IN 1796

Due to the influence of Admiral Sir Thomas Pasley, eminent son of the local family, James was accepted for the Royal Navy and promised the position of Captain's Clerk. A Clerk was employed by and paid by the Captain to assist with the ship's books and other paperwork; the training could eventually lead to the post of Purser. James was appointed to HMS *Tremendous*, a 3rd rate two decker battleship of 74 guns, and joined the ship at Portsmouth on 17th January 1796. In the ship's Muster there is listed an Assistant Surgeon John Bell. They were to meet again seven years later on HMS *Shannon*.

Britain had now been at war with France for three years. In 1792 after the arrest of Louis XVI the hostile reaction of Prussia and Austria led to the outbreak of war. The initial French success resulted in Britain, Spain and the Netherlands forming a coalition with Prussia and Austria. In January 1793 after the execution of King Louis XVI the French Convention annexed the Austrian Netherlands, laid claim to the Scheldt estuary which had previously been granted exclusively to Holland, and declared war on Britain and Holland. In 1795 the French conquered Holland and captured the Dutch fleet. Prussia and Spain, and later Austria, sued for peace and Britain stood alone.

France also laid claim to the overseas possessions of the Dutch East India Company and in particular its settlement at Capetown on Table Bay, Cape of Good Hope. As so much of Britain's prosperity was dependent on overseas trade it was strategically imperative to retain control of the shipping routes to India and the Far East. It was only eight years since the First Fleet had arrived in Australia and the immigrant population was, to a large extent, dependent on supplies arriving from the Cape. Capetown must be held at all costs.

In the spring of 1795 Henry Dundas, Secretary of State for War, had taken a great risk in sending out of the country a considerable part of his much depleted army. It was dispatched to the Cape, without a convoy and during the time of spring gales, under the command of Major-General Craig. He reached False Bay in June, but the Dutch Governor refused to allow him to land. He had to await re-inforcements from home and from St. Helena before he could gain a foothold at Simon's Town and from there he fought his way to Capetown which he entered on 16th September 1795. It was not until the end of November that the news reached London that the shipping route to the East was now safely in British hands.

HMS *Tremendous* sailed from Spithead on 1st May 1796 bound for the Cape of Good Hope. Captain James Aylmer had agreed to take James as his Clerk and promised to rate him Midshipman and his pay on a 3rd rate ship would have been about £2 per lunar month. We find in a later letter that Aylmer had reneged on his promise. He demoted James to the rank of Able Seaman thus relieving himself of the responsibility for paying his wages. How unfair this must have seemed to James and what a disappointing start to his career. Ordinary Seamen were paid 19 shillings per month and an Able Seaman's rate was 24 shillings per month. These rates had remained at that level for well over a century. Furthermore they were only paid in the port of commission so were frequently very much in arrears. As a result of the war there had been a general rise in the cost of living so it was hardly surprising that these appalling conditions of pay eventually led to the Mutiny at Spithead in April 1797.

[To Simon Hyslop, Merchant, Langholm.]

Cape of Good Hope
Simon's Bay 3rd August 1796

Dear Brother,

I have embraced the earliest opportunity of informing you of our safe arrival at the Cape in perfect health, thank God, and hope this will find you all enjoying the same invaluable blessing. We had a very pleasant voyage of 82 days. We sailed from Spithead on Sunday, 1st May, and arrived here on Thursday the 21st July. There was nothing remarkable happened on the voyage. We fell in with several Merchant vessels but they all proved to be neutral ones. We were all very happy on our arrival here in finding it still in the possession of the English, not sure but the Dutch fleet which was said to have sailed before us might have retaken it again. It is a very mountainous uncultivated country about S. Bay, with very few inhabitants, the natives are of a copper colour, the hills are all covered with low shrubbery bushes and all sorts of fine flowers which give the air a most delicious flavour when walking amongst them.

There are only a few houses at S. Bay, inhabited by Dutch people. Their houses are very neat and clean, the natives are all as slaves to them. This is the securest place for the Shipping to lie in winter. (It was the Spring when we arrived here). We expect soon to go to Table Bay on the other side of the Cape, which is a much more fruitful place. There are plenty of oranges, lemons and other fruit growing there. Cape Town is nigh Table Bay. Provisions are very reasonable here, Beef and Mutton are 2d per lb, the sheep here are much like the English Mug-Sheep, except their tail which is remarkably large; at the root it is a foot broad and turns quite small towards the tip. They work mostly with Oxen instead of Horses, generally ten or twelve to a wagon. Fish of all sorts are plentiful here. I have the pleasure of seeing Dr. [Peter] Smith frequently here. When I lived with Mr. Stothart, he had his shop at John Young's, Townfoot, he is surgeon of the Monarch.

The Jupiter with the East India Convoy arrived safe here the day after we arrived. She sailed three weeks before us but was becalmed all that time on the Line, and we had a very good breeze in crossing it. I cannot inform you how long we shall stay at the Cape, but I rather think we shall go to India before we return.

I wish I had a letter of recommendation from Admiral Pasley to Admiral Pringle as there is very little hope of preferment without interest. If you could mention it to the Miss Littles to speak to their uncle or to Mrs. Malcolm I think it could be got, but I will leave it entirely to you to act as you think proper.

Write me soon with all the news since I left Langholm and how you come on with the shop, if trade increases much and how you like your new landlord. Give my love to John and Nanny and Walter [nephew who died in 1801 aged 10] and Maddy and Walter [brother]. Give my kind compliments to Mr. Jamieson when he comes to Langholm. Remember *me to Uncle Simon's family, Thomas', James's, Uncle William Murray, Robert Hotson's family, Wm. Brown, Milntown, Jane Walker and all enquiring friends. Write soon and direct to me H.M.S. Tremendous, Cape of Good Hope or elsewhere. I remain Dear Brother,*

Your affectionate brother,

James Hyslop

P.S. The Trident is just arrived here with her convoy. Wine here is sold at 4d & 6d a bottle.

Tremendous arrived at the Cape on 21st July and as she turned into Simon's Bay saluted Admiral Elphinstone, Flag, with seventeen guns, which salute he returned. She remained at Simon's Bay for some time. On 18th August Captain Aylmer was discharged to the *Moselle*. He was superseded the next day by Captain Charles Brisbane. (Captain Brisbane, later Rear-Admiral, had a distinguished career as the hero of Curaçoa. He received a knighthood K.C.B.).

The Frigate *Moselle* sailed for England on 20th August. It must have given James immense satisfaction to know that Captain Aylmer had been downgraded from a 3rd rate ship to a 5th rate. By May 1797 Aylmer is Captain of *Theseus* and attached to the Mediterranean fleet where Admiral Jervis was in command. Admiral Jervis had a very poor opinion of Aylmer as in May 1797 he wrote "The *Theseus* is an abomination---------If I can prevail on Captain Aylmer to go into the *Captain*, Rear-Admiral Nelson and Captain Miller will soon put *Theseus* to rights." In February 1797 Nelson on the *Captain* had acted on his own initiative and had been instrumental in the defeat of the Spanish Fleet at the Battle of St. Vincent. Later that year Nelson was on board *Theseus* commanding the inshore squadron blockading Cadiz so the transfer had obviously taken place.

On 19th August *Tremendous* captured a ship named Van Tromp and sent on board one commissioned officer, one midshipman and 30 men. For this achievement the crew would be entitled to receive prize money which was a great incentive to capture enemy vessels.

The value of the prize was assessed at the High Court of the Admiralty and there were strict rules for the division of the proceeds. At that time the Captain received three-eighths. The officers, warrant officers and certain petty-officers shared equally another three-eighths and the rest of the crew shared equally the remaining two-eighths. But the Admiralty, with typical bureaucratic dilitariness, was frequently slow to pay up. No doubt James would receive his share eventually.

Captain Brisbane, on his appointment, immediately restored James to the rank of midshipman and on his recommendation James was promoted to HM Sloop *Hope* and was discharged from *Tremendous* on the 22nd August.

CHAPTER 4

1796 to 1800

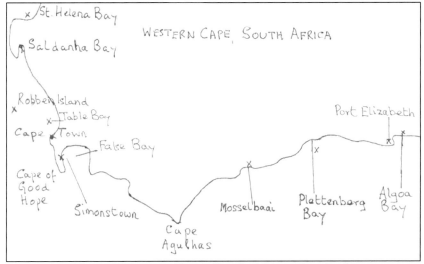

Map of Western Cape, South Africa sketched by the author from the Globetrotter map by Peter Joyce. Copyright New Holland Publishers.

The ship's muster for *HMS Hope,* a Sloop of 14 guns, shows that James joined the ship, "by preferment" on 13th September 1796 and as "Purser per Warrant dated 21st August". This was indeed a generous promotion by Captain Brisbane when one considers how little experience James had had at that point in his career. Perhaps his lack of experience accounts for why he did not receive his official Warrant until July 1800. On the other hand it could have been due to the general dilitariness of the Navy Board.

The *Hope,* originally named *Star,* had been captured from the Dutch in 1795. From August 1796 until November 1797 she was under the command of Captain William Granger. For the first few months the ship patrolled the coast between Simon's Bay and Table Bay and visited Robben Island; the island is now renowned as the place where Nelson Mandela was held for so many years. In July 1797 she sailed east and moored briefly in Plettenburg Bay just west of Port Elizabeth and then continued east to Algoa Bay. There the crew was employed on taking soundings along the bay. At that time there were no published maps of the south coast of Africa so the charts produced by individual ships were of great importance. In September *Hope* sailed back into Mosselbaai and finally returned to Table Bay in October.

The *Hope* anchored in Table Bay for the next three months. In November 1797 Augustus Brine became Captain and remained in command until August 1799. In March 1798 she moved north to Saldanha Bay where she anchored until 9th May when she sailed for St Helena and arrived there on the 26th. Captain Brine writes "At noon, hove to, and sent a Boat on Shore According to the Custom of the Island. The Island saluted us with Eleven Guns and we returned a like number." A few days later he reports "Boarded the America of Boston, bound for Hamburg. Sent the Gunner and three men to take possession of her." Departing from St. Helena on the 27th June she arrived at Simon's Bay on the 18th July. At the end of August *Hope* had a second visit to St. Helena and arrived back at Table Bay on 3rd November.

> *"Hope", Cape of Good Hope,*
> *20th Nov. 1798*

Dear Brother,

I received yours on the 3rd November per the Buffalo, dated the 21st March, 1798, which gave me a great deal of pleasure to hear you were then all well, as I am at present, thank God. I now embrace the opportunity by H.M.S. Stately who is to sail for England with Lord Macartney. I wrote last by the "Crescent", (10th March), since which nothing material has happened. (this letter has been lost although the frigate C*rescent* survived until 1808).

We have been twice at St. Helena since with Despatches to the Governor. It is a small island about 21 miles in circumference and belongs to the E. I. Company. It appears from the sea an entire rock, but in the enclosed parts there are some very fertile valleys. It produces vegetables and fruits of all kinds, but no grain as the vast number of rats which harbour in the rocks destroy it. It is not much inferior in strength (if any) to Gibralter. They have always seven years of provisions on the island for the Garrison in case of siege.

His Majesty's ship, Garland was out on a cruise and was unfortunately lost on the island of Madagascar, but happily the crew were all saved. The Admiral's son was on Board of her. The "Star" Brig was sent to fetch the crew off and should have been here a month ago, it is thought she is taken by some of the French Privateers.

The Admiral is in a very poor state of health, I believe he will return to England shortly, the anxiety for his son makes him worse. I still remain in the Hope. The Purser of the S. Oiscarr was invalided a few weeks ago. The Admiral [Elphinstone] *appointed one of his clerks to her; if Admiral Pringle had been here I make no doubt but he would have promoted me. I wish Admiral Pasley would again recommend me to some of his friends. When we were at St. Helena we detained a ship under*

American Colours and sent her to the Cape in June '98. She has never been heard of since. I believe she would have been a very good prize. It is thought she is lost.

I am glad to hear that Langholm is grown such a flourishing place in the Manufacturing trade. Give my kind love to brothers Walter, John, Nanny and all the children, my Uncles and Aunts and Charles Pasley, let me know in your next what he is doing. If we go to India I shall be very happy to see Thomas Little. Dear Brother, write every opportunity as there is nothing gives me more pleasure than to hear from you. Remember me to Mr. Jamieson and let me know if he keeps his health very well. I shall always be happy to hear of his welfare for his kindness to me when in London.

I remain
Dear Brother
Yours   J. Hyslop

The *Garland* was stationed at the Cape of Good Hope and was cruising in the Indian Ocean searching for French frigates. Her Captain was James Wood. As they approached the coast of Madagascar a French merchant ship was sighted at anchor. Unfortunately as *Garland* was going to investigate she struck a submerged and uncharted rock and such was the damage that she sank before she could be run ashore. The crew escaped in the ship's boats and reached land safely with no loss of life. The French ship, a Merchantman, had also run ashore and Captain Wood was able to capture her. Rescue from Madagascar took longer than expected but they eventually arrived back at the Cape. A Courts Martial was held on HMS *Tremendous* at Table Bay on the 15th December 1798 at which Captain Wood was exonerated for the loss of the *Garland*. The Court commended him and his crew for capturing the French ship and taking prisoner its crew.

On 8th August 1799 James was discharged from the *Hope* on further promotion to the *Camel,* a store ship of 24 guns, stationed at the Cape of Good Hope. He finally receives his Warrant dated 15th July 1800: "James Hyslop of good testimony and late acting in the *Hope*, to be Purser of the *Camel*, former deceased".

There were four Warrant Officers of Ward-room rank, the master, purser, surgeon and chaplain and were appointed by the Navy Board. The purser had to be a man of good education and business acumen. He was responsible for keeping the ship's accounts, issuing victuals and other stores, such as slops (seamen's clothes). As he was responsible for large sums of money the Navy Board required some surety for his honest behaviour. In his next letter James mentions that he has to produce two sureties of £150 pounds each.

He was answerable to the Victualling Board who had to pass his accounts before he received any payment. He was allowed a commission of 12½ per cent on all provisions issued by weight. This sounds a generous allowance but there was often wastage from, for example, a barrel of butter some of which would have melted before it was opened. He was also allowed 10 per cent on tobacco and 5 per cent on slops. In addition he received a small wage according to the Rate of the ship, ranging from 1st rate to 6th rate and under. If a member of the crew died the purser was responsible for auctioning his clothes and possessions. He had to keep a record of the transactions and the amounts were deducted from the purchaser's wages. The money was then sent to the next of kin but the purser was allowed a commission of 5%.

The *Camel* was under the command of Captain John Lee. At the end of August she sailed for Algoa Bay where she remained until November. She was carrying troops and all boats were employed in landing them along with their baggage and stores. On 2nd November

Daniel Cunningham of good testimony to be Boatswain of the Boreas, former (doing duty) deceased

John Brown late Carpenter of the America to be in the Utrecht.

James Wilson (3) late Carpenter of the Niger to be in the Drachterland

James Hyslop of good testimony & late acting in the Hope, to be Purser of the Camel, former deceased.

William Hood . . . . Gunᵣ . . . . . . Camel
Confirmation Admᵗ Sir Roger Curtis, dated 7ᵗ Feb. 1800, former removed to Adamant.

A.   *19.*   *(my*

Joseph Buckingham late Purser of the Chichester to be in the Eclair, former not joined

A.   *19.*   *my*

James's Warrant as Purser.

she sailed to Cape Agulhas, then moored in Hood Bay for a time, visited Darren Island and finally returned to Table Bay on 19th December where she remained until the beginning of April 1800. On 2nd April she sailed for home and had a safe passage. A large proportion of the French Fleet had been destroyed at the Battle of the Nile in 1798 and most of the remainder had retreated to Brest, unable to move thanks to the blockade of the port by the Royal Navy. *Camel* reached Deptford on the 31st July and moored alongside the James Hulk.

Dear Simon,

With pleasure I received yours and am extremely happy to hear that you were all well. I am much afraid that I shall not have the opportunity of seeing you at this time. The "Camel" is gone into Dock a few days ago. She is ordered to be refitted as fast as possible and it is reported she is going out to the Cape again. Since my arrival I have been in town and have been very much put about in procuring an Agent, and am sorry to say I am not quite fixed yet. I have not received any pay since I have been made Purser, as a Purser cannot receive any till he pass his accounts. I have delivered in all my Books and papers for the Hope into the Victualling Office, and am informed it will be two years before my turn comes, as there are so many accounts before me. I don't know how I shall do for money to carry on until my accounts are passed.

The Navy Board requires two securities of about £150 each. I wrote to Mr. Jamieson to see if he would be my security (as he offered before when I was in London). I received for answer that as I was in a seafaring line, and exposed to many dangers, he did not wish to engage. If I had been on shore he would not have had any objections. He also wanted to know the nature of the Bond, which I wrote him, but have not yet had his answer. The nature of the Bond is to secure the Crown from all loss that may arise from the neglect or improper conduct of the Purser. If the ship is lost, or taken by an enemy, the Bond is then annulled.

You were wanting to know the particulars of Capt. Aylmer's behaviour to me. When I joined the Tremendous he promised to make me his clerk and rate me Midshipman, (his Steward was rated Clerk). About a week after we sailed from England for the Cape he disrated me from Midshipman to Able seaman and did not make me clerk as he promised. I remained so till he left the ship. As soon as Capt. Brisbane joined the Tremendous he again rated me Midshipman and behaved with a great deal of civility to me during the time I remained on Board.

I waited upon Mr. John and Charles Pasley. I had the pleasure of seeing the Miss Littles and Miss Malcolm. The Admiral's daughter was there likewise. She is going to be married shortly. [Maria Pasley married Major John Sabine.] The Admiral is expected in Town shortly; both the Miss Littles have promised to speak to him on my behalf. They wished me very much to write to the Admiral again, which I did and have received for answer:

Sir, I have received your letter of the 2nd Inst. in which you solicit my assistance to procure you a ship of a higher rate. I remember your mother well and had a great regard for her and therefore I should be glad to render you any service in my *power, but at present I am so particularly situated by prior applications that I cannot do you any service. If the Camel (as you seem to import) is again ordered to the Cape I can recommend you strongly to the Admiral who commands there and when you return it may be in my power than it is at present.*

I am, Sir,
Yours etc. T. P.

I was very sorry to hear of the death of Uncle James. I had a letter from S. Little [his cousin Simon] *a few days ago dated off Brest Harbour, he is very well. I am sorry to hear of the death of Mr. Irving and daughter. Does George carry on the business as usual? The Miss Littles were asking very kindly after you and Uncle Simon's family and desired to be remembered to you and them. Write me soon with all the news &c.*

I remain &c.,
J. Hyslop

"Camel" at Deptford,
13th. October 1800

Dear Brother,
I have just received your kind letter enclosing me a Draft on London for Twenty Pounds; I am much obliged to you for your attention. I do assure

you it came very seasonable. I see Thomas Telfer is as kind and obliging as ever.

I am very glad to hear you are all well, as I am at present. It will be three weeks or a month before the "Camel" comes out of Dock. I dare say it will be near Christmas before we are ready for sea. I am afraid we are going out again to the Cape. I have secured two securities for the Camel at last, the persons you don't know, the one is a Mr. Lisson, Surgeon in London, the other a Mr. Fothergill in the Bank of England. I could not think of asking Mr. John Pasley after he refused to assist me in 1795. He is a very good man if you do not touch his purse.

I have likewise procured an agent, but he will not advance me any money until my Accounts are passed, without finding him security. Since my last to you I have written to Lord Spencer [First Lord of the Admiralty] stating to him my servitude &c in the Navy. I received for answer from Mr. Harrison, his private secretary, that his Lordship would be glad to see Testimonials of my Character from the Captains I have sailed with, up to the present time. I immediately wrote to Captains Granger and Brine. I received by return of post a letter from Capt. Granger and a certificate from Capt. Brine. (A copy of both I have sent you.) Capt. Lee desired me to write out any certificate I pleased and he would sign it. I enclosed them to his Lordship and received for answer from Mr. Harrison, saying that his Lordship had set down my name on his list of candidates for advancement in my line of service, but that his Lordship could not give me immediate expectation of it. I am afraid his Lordship's list of candidates is a very long one. I have now done all I can. I must wait with patience the event and trust the rest to Providence.

There was a very dreadful fire broke out at Wapping this day week which consumed a great many houses and several lives are said to be lost. I happened to be going up the town at the time. I passed it about 9 o'clock in the morning, it was then raging with great fury. It had just then caught hold of a very large Cooperage where was a great quantity of Wood, Hoops and Stores. It continued burning till next morning when it was got under. It was a most shocking scene to see. There was a great number of Fire Engines but the lanes were so narrow they had not room to play on the fire. The loss is computed to be about Two hundred thousand pounds.

A Copy of Capt. Granger's Letter

Dear Hyslop,

Yours of the 9th Inst. I have just received and according to your request have returned you an answer. Likewise I have left blank paper sufficient for you to fill up the certificate and have to request that you will let it be as handsome a one as possible, for you are most undoubtedly entitled to it. I would have done it myself, but from not exactly knowing the whole form have therefore only put my signature. I am in hopes of getting a ship soon and should I be able to make interest enough to get you with me, I dare say you will have no objections, at some time it would give me much pleasure. I hope my worthy friend Capt. Lee is well. I have been in expectation of hearing from him, tell him I wrote about three weeks since requesting a little Cape news. Brine I find came home with you. Poor Mrs. Linzee I am sorry to see by the papers is dead. Mr. Fullerton tells me that the L'Oisea was found to be in a much better state than expected and is to be kept in Commission. I have to return your thanks for the very correct manner in which you kept everything that was necessary for my Agent passing my Accounts. They have passed for some time and I have received my pay.

I remain, Dear Hyslop,
Yours truly,
Wm. Granger (signed)

I do hereby certify that the conduct of Mr. James Hyslop (during the time of my commanding H.M. Sloop Hope from the 27th day of November 1797 to the 9th day of August 1799) was such as to merit my entire satisfaction whether in his official capacity as a Purser, or a Gentleman, and I do further certify that I received a good character of him from his former Captain.

Given under my hand this 10th day of September, 1800 (Signed) Augt. Brine

Both Capt. Granger and Brine are unemployed at present. I hope they will soon get a ship each, for they are both two worthy young men. Granger is in hopes of getting one soon. I hope I will get again with him. Write me soon with all the news about Langholm as every little trifling thing from that quarter gives me pleasure. Give my Compliments to John, Walter, Nanny and all the children and all enquiring friends. I remain, Dear Simon

Your affectionate brother,

J. Hyslop.

Captain Granger was appointed in January 1801 to the *Hyaena*. Later in his Naval career he became a Rear-Admiral and after a few more years a Vice-Admiral. Captain Brine also had a successful career, eventually being appointed Rear-Admiral.

Camel remained in dock at Deptford for the rest of the year and James continued to be employed as Purser. In this capacity he would continue to live on board ship so would not have to find and pay for lodgings.

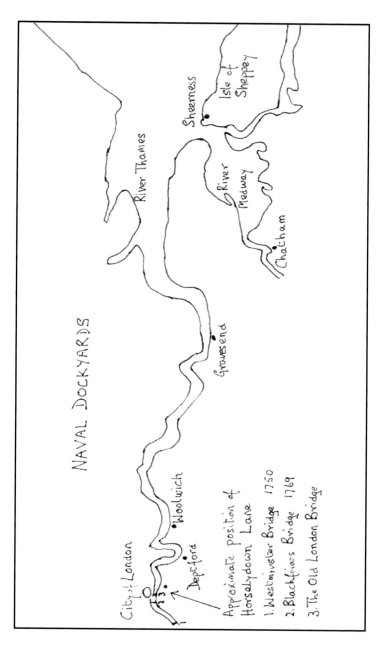

Naval Dockyards, rough sketch to show position.

CHAPTER 5

THE MISSING YEARS

There are no further letters from James until December 1803. No doubt he had been in touch with his brother Simon during that time but, unfortunately, no letter has survived.

In his last letter James was under the impression that they would be returning to the Cape, so the news that *Camel* was to go the West Indies, totally new territory for him, would be a pleasant surprise.

On 17th January 1801 the ship's company mustered and next day *Camel* moved down river to Woolwich. She was lashed alongside the Rainbow Hulk for the next week, then, gradually working down river, she moored in Long Reach where she stayed for a month while taking stores on board. By the beginning of March she was in the Downs and on the 5th sailed for Spithead arriving there three days later. A month later *Camel* set sail on 5th April. At the end of May she reached Carlisle Bay in Barbados and arrived at Port Royal, Kingston, Jamaica on 30th June where she remained until the end of July.

According to the ship's muster James is discharged from *Camel* on 20th July 1801 to *HMS Abergavenny* but this statement was incorrect and led to frustrating and unproductive research. His wages on discharge, after various deductions, amounted to £27.3.4d but were not paid to his agent until January 1805 by which time he was a prisoner in France.

Fortunately a letter from James's younger brother Walter gave news of him. Walter was a joiner to trade and in the autumn of 1801 had arranged to sail to Jamaica to work on a sugar plantation. On the night before he was due to depart from Langholm he visited all his friends to bid them farewell. No doubt it was a convivial evening and perhaps he had one *deoch an doris* (one for the road) too many. On his way home he failed to see an open drain, fell in and broke his leg. Of course he could not sail as arranged and many were the lamentations at this misfortune. However, the lamentations soon turned to thankfulness that a benign Providence had been looking after him. Word came that the ship on which he should have sailed had been lost at sea with no survivors. Walter, after recovering from his broken leg, eventually sailed from Liverpool to Jamaica on the *Lord Rodney*, a merchantman, under the command of Captain Turnbull.

Kingston, 1st February 1802

Dear Brother,

I now take this opportunity of letting you know that I have got well to Kingston after a long passage of 69 days. We sailed from Liverpool on the 26th September in company with another ship called the Mary Anne, but we parted company that same night in a gale of wind and never saw her afterwards. When we got to Madeira we heard that she had been there but sailed the day before our arrival.

We had very coarse weather for three weeks after we left Liverpool, very high winds and much rain and which was worse the wind contrary the whole time. We were a long time in the Bay of Biscay which is a bad place for Privateers. We saw two or three that were supposed to be such, but they never durst come within 5 or 6 leagues as our ship had so much the appearance of a Frigate.

October 19 we spoke to an English Frigate who told us it was peace which was not believed by any of the ship's company as we had then only been three weeks out. Next day we spoke to one under Russian colours, had been 15 days from Plymouth bound for Lisbon, who told us the same.

We arrived Madeira October 24 and took on 80 pipes of wine and unloaded coals. I can give little or no account of Madeira as none of us was ever ashore. We lay about two miles from the wharf and all the wine came to us in boats. It appears to be a very fertile place for fruits of all kinds, but it is a very mountainous country, any that we saw of it, and bushes green on the top of the mountains. We sailed from Madeira Nov. 4 and had a very pleasant passage to Kingston of 31 days. We neither had a gale of wind nor a shower of rain but we had plenty before.

I am now engaged with a Master in Kingston for 12 months for £100 Currency, Bed, Board and Washing and am now working about 3 miles in the country which is a very good thing for anyone when they first come to the place until they get seasoned to the place.

The man I am with is from Hull in Yorkshire. Has been here for 16 years. He has another white man besides myself and 27 Negroes all his own. I am mostly at the country myself with 10 or sometimes 12 of the Negroes. The work is very easy as the Negroes do all the coarse work and the hours we work are from 7 in the morning till 4 in the afternoon which is the hour we dine, but have what we call first and second breakfast at 8 and 2.

Captain Turnbull behaved to me more like a brother than a man I had never seen. Although I wrought my passage I did almost nothing unless assisting the Carpenter sometimes in the day and kept no watch in the night. He said he would excuse me as Joiners are not used to being out of bed in the night. When we got to Kingston he told me to make the ship my home and not leave her till I got a Master, for I would find it very expensive living ashore, which I thought very kind of him. Living is very high here. One cannot go to a common lodging house and get a tea breakfast under 5 shillings and every other thing as dear in proportion.

I hear James is sailed for England about a fortnight ago. Although we were within 6 miles of one another for 5 weeks I could never find him, until I heard he had been at the wharf, where our ship lay, enquiring for me, but she was gone before that and there was none could give him any account of me. As soon as I heard I took a boat and went down to Port Royal, a distance of 6 miles, where all the King's ships are lying and enquired among them. I found he had been on board La Topaze Frigate but had left her only two days before which I was so much disappointed. Ask the name of the ship he has gone on and when you write let me know.

I have now been here 8 weeks and I thank God has kept my health very well. This is a good place for a tradesman if he keeps his health but if sick he will get very few visits from a Doctor for at £20 or £30 their bills come very high. Dear Simon, you will no doubt think I have been very careless to be two months without writing but being in the country I missed the first Packet and it only goes once a month. I hope you will not be so long in writing after you receive this. Let me know all the news from Langholm. I hear you have got the Meal and every other thing is very cheap.

I like this place very well and have got a very agreeable man for a Master and plenty of good meat and drink. I find no inconvenience at all from the heat although I believe this is the coolest time of the year.

Let me know if there are any of my old acquaintances in town or country has got married this Winter. Give my compliments to John, Nanny and the children and all enquiring friends. You may let John Thomson know that I have forwarded his son John's letter as soon as I landed here, which I hope he would receive as it is no great distance from here. Let me know if William T. is still in Liverpool yet. When I parted with him he told me not to write to him as he would not be in Liverpool. He intended coming to Jamaica in the spring. If he is not gone give him my Direction as I would be very happy to meet him here. You may continue me on the Friendly Society if the time is not out before you receive this. I hope I shall not stand much in need of it but if I should I have got no Articles. If you could send that single Article that speaks of a member being abroad it might be done with little trouble.

Which is all from your affectionate brother,

W. Hyslop

When you write direct to me to the care of Mr. Robert Soadon, Carpenter, Rosemary Lane, Kingston, Jamaica.

The Frigate *La Topaze* had been captured from the French and in January 1801 was re-fitting at Portsmouth. On 12th February she sailed in convoy to the West Indies and by June she was moored at Port Royal, Jamaica. The Purser on this voyage was a James Bellamy, but he, poor man, according to the Ship's Muster, had the misfortune to be Discharged Dead on June 17th. He was followed briefly by an A. Stewart and then on 6th August 1801, James Hyslop became Purser, per warrant. This was indeed a stroke of good fortune for James. A Frigate was a 5th rate ship and considerably more prestigious than a store ship and he would of course receive a higher rate of pay.

La Topaze spent August and early September patrolling the coast of Jamaica, ensuring that no enemy ships were in the vicinity, after which she moored at Port Royal for several weeks. On 6th November she sailed west and arrived at Grand Cayman three days later. December was spent at sea and she arrived back at Grand Cayman on the 31st, and then returned to Port Royal where she arrived on 18th January 1802.

According to the Pay Book for *La Topaze* James was discharged on 18th January to join *La Seine* as Purser. His wages, on discharge, were recorded as £3.13.6d and £5.3.8d but once again

52

there was considerable delay in payment. More than three years elapsed and payment was not until the 29th April 1805.

The Frigate *La Seine,* had been captured from the French in June 1798. She had been sighted off the French coast by the *Jason*, the *Mermaid* and the *Pique,* the captain of the latter being David Milne. All three ships gave chase and the Pique was the first to attack but had her main-topmast shot away. After repairs she again gave chase but she and *Jason* and *La Seine* all ran aground, almost simultaneously, and as *La Seine* lost all her masts she was forced to surrender. *Jason* and *La Seine* were refloated but *Pique* was a total loss.

David Milne, born 1763 in Musselburgh, entered the Navy as a Midshipman in 1779. In the early years of the Napoleonic Wars he gained considerable experience in various engagements in the West Indies. In January 1796, he was given command of *La Pique*, a Frigate which had been captured by the *Blanche* on which Milne was Second-Lieutenant. At the Courts Martial held to investigate the loss of La Pique Captain Milne was acquitted. *La Seine* was refitted and in 1799 Captain Milne was appointed to her command.

La Seine had been at Port Royal since the beginning of 1802 and James joined the ship as Purser, per Warrant, on 19th January. She sailed next day in convoy escorted by the Frigate *Apollo.* During the voyage home Captain Milne had to contend with appalling weather conditions. After nine days the ship was making twelve inches of water per hour and the forward pumps were working continously. Strong gales carried away the main top gallant yard and squalls and rain continued for several days. Not until the 12th February were the carpenters able to fit a new top mast. The weather continued in the same vein throughout the voyage and it says much for Captain Milne's superb seamanship that *La Seine* arrived safely at Chatham on 31st March. The crew was paid off on 15th April.

CHAPTER 6

SHIPWRECKED

In the autumn of 1801 the preliminaries of peace between France, England and Austria were negotiated and the Treaty of Amiens, which finally brought peace, was signed at the end of March 1802.

The Peace of 1802, although a welcome respite, was fragile. Britain needed peace for trade. Napoleon, with dreams of dominating the whole of Europe, required time to build up his forces. Later that year Napoleon made himself First Consul for life and was now in full control of France. By November he was active in Italy and annexed Piedmont. He was also insisting that Britain should return Malta to the Tsar of Russia. In the spring of 1803 he occupied Switzerland. Napoleon's ambition knew no bounds and his intent was to control the whole of Europe. The French had for the moment cowed the Continent into a passive acceptance of their mastery and Britain stood alone.

It was now obvious that Napoleon's next move was the invasion of Britain. He assembled his vast army near the English Channel but first he had to build a fleet of small boats with which to transport his troops. He must also gain Naval control of the Channel. On the 16th May 1803 Britain declared war on France. Throughout 1803 and 1804 the Royal Navy kept up a constant blockade of the Channel ports, the coast of the Netherlands and the French naval bases at Brest and Rochefort on the Atlantic coast. In order to do this effectively the ships had to patrol very close to land, a difficult task for ships under sail, and inevitably many had the misadventure of running aground or being blown ashore in a gale.

La Seine remained at Chatham throughout 1802 and refitting was not completed until the end of May 1803. James continued as Purser during this time at Chatham but in April 1803 he was temporarily replaced by Richard Sinnet. Was James having some time off? Perhaps to enjoy a visit to his brothers in Langholm? Who knows? He returned to the ship as Purser on May 26th and *La Seine* began Wages and Sea Victualling at Chatham on the 30th. The ship's complement of men was 284 and David Milne resumed command. Preparations continued and she finally sailed on July 5th.

Captain Milne had been instructed to join the blockade of the river Elbe and *La Seine* was progressing in that direction when, due to strong gales, she was blown off course. In attempting to regain her station in the blockade she was steering along the Dutch coast when she ran onto a sandbank off Terschelling Island, north-east of Texel Island.

Captain Milne, in his report to the Admiralty dated 23rd July 1803, said that on the morning of the 21st July, due to the ignorance (or wilfulness) of the Pilots, the ship had run onto a sandbank off Schelling Island. The Master had previously reported a depth of only fourteen fathoms and Captain Milne had repeatedly told the Pilots not to go any nearer to land but they had insisted that there was no danger. Very soon the ship struck the ground and after beating over the obstruction for some minutes stuck fast.

Two ships under neutral colours were sighted, distress guns were fired and these two ships came to their aid. The initial attempts to free her concentrated on passing hawsers to the ships nearby and hauling her off. When this failed, guns and stores were heaved overboard and anchors taken out. At the next high tide *La Seine* made considerable way towards the vessels but the wind got up and heavy seas damaged the ship still further. The ship was leaking badly due to the pounding she had taken and the rudder was unshipped. The leaks became uncontrollable and the water reached above the cockpit deck. Captain Milne discussed the situation with all the officers and it was decided that nothing could be done to save her.

The crew were all rescued and the frigate abandoned, being set on fire by the last men to leave. At the Courts Martial on 4th August the two pilots, James Waite and Robert Horsburgh, were both found guilty and sentenced to serve two years in Marshalsea prison.

James must surely have written home about his unfortunate experience but any letter has not survived. However worse was to follow. His next appointment as Purser was to HMS *Shannon*, a frigate of 36 guns, under the command of Captain Edward Leveson Gower. James joined the ship at Chatham on 20th September 1803. According to *Shannon's* Muster Book wages for the crew began on 13th September and Sea Victualling on the 19th. James would be pleasantly surprised to find that the Surgeon was John Bell with whom he had sailed on HMS *Tremendous*. As a surgeon John was classed as a warrant officer on a par with the master, purser and chaplain.

John Bell, son of Joseph Bell and Ann Mandeville, was born in 1771 in the village of Kirkoswald, near Penrith, Cumberland. In the ship's muster for *Tremendous* he is said to be from Carlisle where he may have received his medical training as an apprentice to a Carlisle doctor. I can find no record of him at either Glasgow or Edinburgh Universities and it seems unlikely that he would go as far afield as St. Andrew's, Aberdeen, Oxford or Cambridge. As James and John were both from the same part of the country they probably had many interests, and possibly aquaintances, in common.

On 12th October *Shannon* set sail for the French coast. Captain Gower was under orders to blockade the Port of Le Havre and his station extended from Cape de Caux, on which lies St. Valery en Caux, to Cape Barfleur.

(This town became famous in 1940 when the 51st Highland Division was surrounded and forced to surrender to the invading German army. Their route march to prison camp was as horrendous as any similar event during Napoleonic times.)

In December 1803 violent gales hit the Channel which made it difficult for Captain Gower to maintain his station. He had also been obliged to send his Pilot to the *Pluto* whose Master was sick.

Captain Gower and the Master then had to rely on their own knowledge and experience of the coastline. On 10th December *Shannon* hit a submerged reef near La Hougue on the north-east coast of the Cherbourg peninsula. For the second time in less than six months James was shipwrecked.

Caen in Normandy
19th December 1803

Dear Brother,

Before this you will no doubt have heard of our unfortunate shipwreck, which happened on the 10th December at ¼ past 8 in the evening near La Hogue [sic]. *We were immediately marched from La Hogue to this place, about sixty miles, where we arrived on the 17th, we begin our march again on Friday for Verdun where we are to remain. The Minerve's officers are there.*

Thank God I have kept my health very well and am happy to say we are treated very civilly. I hope it will not be long before there is an exchange of Prisoners. Give my compliments to Brother John, Nanny and all our friends and tell them not to be the least uneasy about me as I am as comfortable as the circumstances of the case will permit.

Mr. Bell has written to his brother in London [this must be his elder brother Joseph as his younger brother, James, died in 1791] *desiring him to mention in the Papers that all the Officers are well.*

I remain, Dear Brother, Your affectionate

57

brother, J. Hyslop.

The following is an extract from a letter written by Captain Gower to the Admiralty from Caen in Normandy, dated 22nd December 1803.

"With the deepest regret I have to inform your Lordship that the Shannon run on Shore between La Hougue and Cape Barfleur about half past eight on the night of the 10th soon after high water, within sight of the nearby Battery which commenced firing at us. Every exertion was made during the night to get her off without success. By next morning the Hull, battered with shot, was leaking badly, and the Fore and Main masts were shot away. Three men had been killed and eight wounded. There was no prospect of getting the ship off and the guns continued to rake her. The French then brought down field pieces so that any further resistance seemed pointless."

Further information is found in the official report which states that with heavy seas and high winds *Shannon* ran onto a reef.

The report continues:-

"In order to lighten the ship some anchors, stores, and upper deck guns were thrown overboard and the mizen mast was cut away. Daylight revealed that she had run aground near the French coast between Cap Barfleur and La Hougue and the French were bringing up further field pieces. Boats were lowered in an attempt to kedge her off and she finally floated, but with shot holes in the hull she

was very low in the water. Again she ran aground. The French continued with their onslaught all day, shattering the rigging and both remaining masts were shot through and the hull riddled At eight-thirty that evening she surrendered."

The *Merlin* sloop returned to the site six days later and burnt the wreck to prevent the French making any use of the remains.

The *Minerve*, whose officers were already at Verdun, was part of the squadron blockading Cherbourg and in fog on 3rd July 1803 she had run aground within sight of two French forts and two gunbrigs. They all attacked with such force and damaged her to such an extent that she was finally forced to surrender. Captain Jahleel Brenton was detained at Verdun for almost three years until released on an exchange. The rest of the crew were prisoners until the end of the war.

Verdun,
25th January, 1804

Dear Brother,

I wrote you on the 19th December from Caen, which I hope you have received safe. We set off on the 22nd December and arrived here the 10th January, in very good health thank God. There are about 400 English Prisoners here, viz. Officers of Men of War, Masters of Merchantmen and Gentlemen that were detained in France at the time the war broke out; the sailors are all at Valenciennes or Sedan.

Thank God, I never had my health better in my life and am as comfortable as we can expect, considering being Prisoners. We have the liberty of walking a league round the town, by applying to the General for leave to go out at the gates. I have not troubled him as yet, having had walking enough lately. We marched between 4 & 500 miles, my poor feet were in a sad pickle the first two or three days. We had continual rain the first 14 days which made the roads very bad; we were over the tops of our shoes every step.

We stopped at Caen five days; by that time my feet got quite well again and continued so to the end of our journey. Before we got to our journey's end I thought no more of 26 or 28 miles a day than I used to think of going over to the Kerr. When I return again to England, I mean to save the expense of coach hire by walking from London to Langholm.

Let me hear from you as soon as you receive this with all the news and what are become of the houses, if they are sold or not. Give my kind compliments to Brother John, Nanny and children and all our friends. Let me know when you heard from Walter if he was well. When you write, direct to me, English Prisoner at Verdun, Department of the Meuse, and enclose it in a cover to Monsr. Perregaux, Banker, Paris, and pay the inland postage. Let me know what is become of Walter Corrie, he may think himself very fortunate he did not get into the Shannon. Remember me to all enquiring friends.

I remain Your affectionate Brother ,
J. Hyslop

When you see Mr. Bell, you may let him know his brother is very well.

After leaving from Caen on 22nd December their march of twenty days took them through Lisieux, Rouen, Gournay-en-Bray, Beauvais, Clerment, Campiègne, Soissons, Reims, Charleville, before arriving at Verdun. James was now Prisoner number 391

Monsieur Perregaux was a leading banker with banks in both Paris and London and a friend of the French foreign minister. He had English staff working in Paris and, due to the Minister's influence, they were allowed to remain at the bank.

Walter Corrie, aged 20 years, was listed in November 1803 as an Able Seaman on board the troopship *HMS Leopard.* He is said to be from Scotland so it seems reasonable, in view of James's concern for his welfare, to assume he was from the Langholm area although I have not been able to find him in any parish records. It is possible that he could be connected with the Mr. Corrie who is mentioned in subsequent letters.

Walter joined the Navy as a Volunteer in 1803 and was indeed unfortunate on his first voyage. In the ship's muster for *HMS Leopard,* a troopship, there is a note *"wrecked on the late La Seine".* He was still serving on the *Leopard* when it was wrecked in June 1814 near the Isle of Anticosta in the St. Lawrence river.

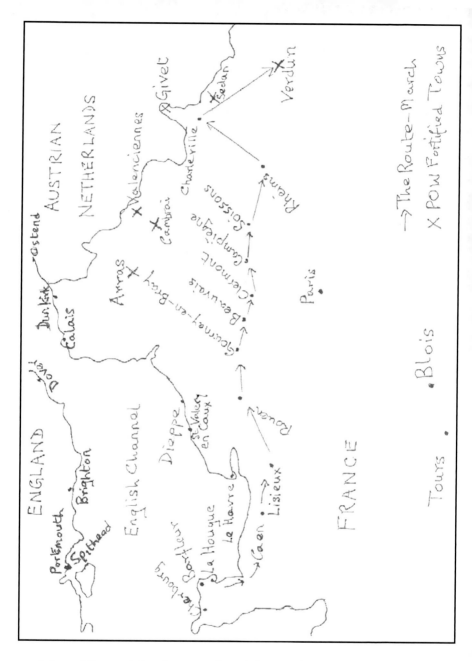

Map of Route-March, reproduced from information in Samuel Robinson's log book.

CHAPTER 7

VERDUN 1804

Along the eastern border of France there were numerous fortified towns built originally to protect the country from any invading forces. However, when France became the belligerent country and extended her territory eastwards into Bavaria, the Austrian Netherlands, Holland and eventually across Europe, these towns were no longer required as a defence. Enclosed by high walls and entered through strong gateways they were ideal places in which to house the prisoners of war.

Verdun, an ancient fortified town situated on the river Meuse and with well built houses, was the place chosen by Napoleon to be the depot for Officers and Gentlemen. The Officers were separated from their Men in order to prevent them from becoming a rallying point for any insurrection.

The main entrance to Verdun is through the eastern gate, named La Porte Chaussée, a massive structure built in the fifteenth century. Above the Porte there is a strong gatehouse which was used as a prison. There was also the main prison which was at the Citadel, or fortress, situated on a hill west of the town and surrounded by its own high walls and from which escape was almost impossible.

During the short period of peace many wealthy members of the aristocracy had flocked to France, partly from curiosity to see the changes in the country after the revolution, and also to enjoy the delights of Paris.

At the outbreak of war Napoleon decreed that these tourists were to be taken prisoner. English civilians found in any country occupied by his troops were also to be imprisoned and all English property or merchandice confiscated. This was the first time in any war that civilians had been detained. These détenus were regarded as

La Porte Chausée, Verdun, photograph June 2003

Gentlemen and were sent to Verdun. In addition people who had been employed by French businesses were also detained there.

Prisoners were billeted on the local population but had to pay for their accommodation and sustenance. As Officers and Gentlemen they were on Parole d'Honneur which theoretically implied they were free to walk around the town and pursue any activities that they wished but were on their honour not to attempt an escape. The Commandant of the town lived at the Citadel and prisoners were required to attend there to sign their parole agreement. They had to report regularly to the Town Hall but the frequency depended on the rank of the individual. The French officials were not averse to bribery so that anyone with sufficient means could reduce the frequency of reporting.

Original gate of the Citadel, photograph June 2003.

The giving of one's word of honour was a serious undertaking and to break parole was considered a heinous offence by both French and British authorities. Anyone doing so was dealt with severely; however, every law can be circumvented!

Amongst the officers were all the young midshipmen, in training to be officers, many of whom were just exuberant teenagers. They reasoned, justifiably, that if they could misbehave sufficiently for the French to imprison them in the Citadel then the French had broken their promise of freedom in the town. Therefore they on their part were no longer bound by parole. Many a daring escape took place and a few were even successful. Those unfortunates who were recaptured were sent to the infamous, notorious and appropriately named prison at Bitche where conditions were appalling and escape virtually impossible.

Verdun,
2nd May 1804

Dear Brother,

Yours of the 14th March I have just received which gives me great pleasure to find you were then all well, as I am at present, thank God. I am likewise happy to hear that Walter was well by the last account, and that Nanny and my little namesake are doing well. [nephew James was born in January 1804] The houses are very long in being sold. I am very sorry I cannot lend you any assistance in respect to the purchasing of them, having been so very unfortunate lately. Has John got the garden finished yet ? I am sorry I cannot lend him a hand with it this season.

I little thought this time twelvemonth I should be here working in the garden. The people with whom I lodge have got a fine large Garden with all sorts of fruit. I spend a good deal of my time in it. Mr. Bell and I lodge both in one house, the people are remarkably civil. We have been very fortunate in respect to lodgings. When you see or write to Mr. Bell you may let him know his brother is very well.

It is a famous wine country about Verdun, the town is surrounded with vineyards. The wine is very reasonable here, altho' they have had but very indifferent crops these two or three years past.

There is every appearance at present of a plentiful crop.

We have horse races two or three times a month, made by the English gentlemen here. I belong to a club which consists of 120 members, we have all the French papers, the "Argus", an English paper printed in Paris, with all the periodical publications &c, upon the whole the time passes away very pleasantly.

There is an English lady here at present who married a Mr. Rudden. I believe she is a distant relative of Mr. Malcolm's family, her maiden name is Petrie, she married in India.

Let me hear from you soon with all the news about Langholm and how the manufactories come on; and if John and Alexr. Hotson have sold all the muslin and if they lost much by it.

[It seems strange that a builder was dealing in muslin. Perhaps Alexander was financing his brother, a thread manufacturer, in a new venture.]

Let me know if Captains Pultney and Charles Malcolm are employed. Give my compliments to Brother John, Nanny, children and all our friends. I am sorry to hear that S. Murray [his cousin Simon] is not any better yet.

Direct to me English Prisoner, Verdun, Department of the Meuse, France and pay the inland postage. You need not enclose it to Mr. Perregaux. Remember me to all enquiring friends.

Ask Nanny how she would like a French lady for a sister.

> I remain, Dear Simon,
> Your affectionate brother,
> J. Hyslop

Verdun

10th October 1804

Dear Brother,

I again embrace the opportunity of writing to you. I wrote to you on the 2nd May, but have not had an answer. The last I had from you was dated the 14th March. I am very well at present, thank God, and will be happy to hear you and all friends are the same. For the future you must write me every six weeks, or two months at most, and not wait for answers, the conveyance is so very irregular; and I will do the same. If you have received mine of the 2nd May answer it again as I dare say the other is lost. What sort of crops have you had in the North? Have they been good in general? When did you hear from Walter? Is he likely to remain in Jamaica for some time? What wages has he now? I hope John has been very busy this summer, what new houses has he built?

*Typical old house of the Napoleonic era;
photograph June 2003.*

They have just begun the Vintage here, it is remarkably good, they have not had such a one since '85. The wine is fallen full two thirds since our arrival in France. We have very excellent old wine for sixpence a bottle. The Lady with whom we lodge will have about thirty pieces this year, each piece [pièce, cask or barrel] runs about 19 doz. Last year she had only half a piece and for several years past not more than six or seven pieces.

Mr. [John] Bell, Mr. [Alex.] Eckford, Marine Officer, and myself have messed together ever since we came here, and about a week ago we had a new messmate joined us, which was Mrs. Eckford from England. She was only 14 days from Gravesend. She is a very pleasant young Lady, it will be much more pleasant for us to have a lady to manage matters, although we made it out very well before as Mr. Eckford's servant was a very good cook and managed matters very well. Mr. E. was quite surprised as he had a letter from her a short while before saying she could not procure passports.

There was a Mrs. Bruce, (a Captain of a Merchantman's Lady) came over with her. Let me know if Walter Corrie is still in the Leopard and if he is likely to get forward in the service. Poor fellow he was very unfortunate at first setting out. I hope he will be more fortunate for the future.

Write me a long letter with all the news about Langholm, Deaths, Births and Marriages &c. Give my compliments to Brother John, Nanny &

Children, all our friends at the Kerr, Auchenrivock, Hagg, Terrona, Carrickrigg &c & let me know how Simon Murray is. I hope he is quite well again. Remember me likewise to the Revd. Messrs. Martin and Jardine, Dr. Moffat, Col. Murray, Dr. Douglas, Robert Hotson & John Hotson's family, Mr. & Mrs. Brown, Milntown, the Goodwife, Mrs Laidlay, James Carruthers' family, & all enquiring friends.

I remain Dear Brother,
Your very affectionate brother,
J. Hyslop

Direct to me "English Prisoner at Verdun, Department of the Meuse, France" you need not enclose it to Mr. Perregaux.

CHAPTER 8

VERDUN 1805 - 1807

Verdun, 9th May 1805

Dear Brother,

I dare say you will be surprised at not hearing from me before this. I delayed it on account of a report we have had here for some time past of a speedy exchange. I assure you I expected to be in England before this, but now I am afraid it is all at an end. I think now there is every prospect of remaining here during the War.

I am quite busy at present working in the Garden, as you must know we have hired one for the season, gardening is quite the rage amongst the English at present. I should be very happy not to be allowed to remain to enjoy the fruits of our labour. We have got plenty of fruit trees, berry bushes and vines in it. You may be looking out for a pipe of wine by and by.

You may tell Nanny when I return I will teach her to cook some nice delicate French dishes; there is one in particular which I have eaten frequently, and which I dare say she will like very much, it is made from an animal called Grenouille*, besides a number of more dishes quite as nice and savoury.

When did you hear from Walter? I hope he is well. When you write remember me to him. Let me know what are his wages now, if he has had them advanced lately. In your last you said you did not wish to write often for the postage, not knowing how I was off for money. [In those days the recipient of the letter was responsible for paying the postage.]

I am happy to say I am very well off in that respect, as the Admiralty has given permission to all the Officers whilst prisoners to draw their personal pay, and that, together with the French pay** does pretty well, so I hope you will not let that be a hindrance for the future, as it always gives me great pleasure to hear from you.

I hope you and all friends have been well since I heard from you last. What prospects has John this season? Will he have plenty of work? In my last letters I desired you to let me know how John and Alex. Hotson came on with the muslin, you had either overlooked it or forgot to mention it in your last. In your next let me know all about it.

Give my compliments to John, Nanny and the children. I hope the children have been very good since I went away. Tell them if I hear they have I will bring them something very fine when I return from France. I hope to find them all good scholars. Remember me to all enquiring friends.

I remain, Dear Brother yours, J. Hyslop

*Frog **37½Livers, a Liver [Livre] is 10d. [4 new pence]

James was indeed fortunate in his level of pay from the French government. The amount paid to a prisoner depended on rank, a captain in the Royal Navy receiving £4 per month, whereas a midshipman received 25 shillings. At the rate which James quotes in his letter he would receive 375d which is £1.11.3d. (For those readers who are unfamiliar with pre-decimal coinage there were 12 pence, written as d for denarius, in a shilling and 20 shillings in one pound sterling.) Amongst the prisoners at Verdun the variation in living standards was immense. The détenues who were wealthy could send home for more funds whereas a ship's captain in the Merchant Service was not so fortunate. Whether he was regarded as an officer at all depended on the tonnage of his ship as did his level of remuneration from the French. If the tonnage was over 80 then the captain was an officer with pay of 25 livres per month. If the ship's tonnage was less than 80 the captain was classed as an ordinary seaman who received only three farthings per day or 1s 10½d per month. This was certainly not sufficient to live on and many merchant navy officers were reduced to penury.

The French refused to allow the British government to assist in any way but voluntary donations were allowed. In July 1803 Lloyd's Patriotic Fund was established to provide relief for prisoners of war, wounded soldiers and sailors and also for their widows and orphans. Thousands of pounds were raised and distributed throughout the war years. This money was a welcome lifeline to those who were poverty stricken.

As there were so many young midshipmen and young children at Verdun the committee of prisoners decided to set up an English school. James was amongst those who contributed to the cost. This is hardly surprising as in later letters he is so vehement about the importance of a good education.

Verdun, 9th October 1805

Dear Simon

Yours of the 12th June came safe to hand, by which I am happy to find you were then all well as I am at present. It is currently reported that the Prisoners of War are to be sent to another depot, but where I know not, some say Lille, others Cambrai, but it is all conjecture.

There were about a hundred detenus sent to Valenciennes last week, they only had one days notice, so I suppose we shall be sent off with as little, but not to be taken unawares I have got my marching Shoes and Knapsack &c put in order, so that I may be able to march at a moments notice. Oh, I wish it were to England. We are in great hopes that the Continental War will bring about an exchange.

We have had famous races this last summer. An English gentleman here (Mr. Hume) got a fine English blood horse; another gentleman (Mr. Gold) laid Mr. H. a wager of one thousand pounds last May, that he would find a horse before the 5th Sept. that would beat Mr. H's. Mr. Gold got one before the day appointed and during the interval there were bets laid to the amount of four thousand pounds. There were several Ladies and Gentlemen from Paris to see this famous race. There were betwixt 70 and 80 carriages on the race course. Mr. Gold lost the wager.

The summer has been very wet and cold, there will be very little wine this season in consequence of it. You sent me a famous budget of news last letter, some of which you thought you had mentioned before, but you had not, tell Mary Hyslop I was *sorry I had not the pleasure of dancing at her wedding.* [Mary at The Kerr married John Beattie.] *I was glad to hear that Walter was well the last letter you had from him, remember me kindly to him when you write. I am sorry to hear Simon Murray is never any better. Write me soon and direct as usual, if we are gone from Verdun it will be forwarded to me. As we are likely to be separated from the detained, say <u>English Prisoner of War</u>. Remember me kindly to Brother John, Nanny and the children and all enquiring friends.*

I remain, Dear Simon,
Your affectionate Brother   J. Hyslop

P.S. John was wanting to know how much I put into the manufactory. I think it was £30 from he & I.

The Mr. Gold who lost the wager is Dr. Valentine Goold, or Gould, a détenue, who had been working in France when hostilities broke out. He appears to have been a flamboyant character and a gambler. On one occasion the owner of a gaming house, a Monsieur Balbi, had refused to hand over Goold's winnings. Such an insult could only be settled in one way. The duel took place next day and Goold shot away part of Balbi's calf. Needless to say, Goold was arrested and sent to the infamous prison at Bitche. When Balbi recovered, and to prove that he too was a gentleman, he went to Paris and spoke to the Minister of War and secured the release of Goold, returning with him to Verdun.

Valentine Goold was released from Verdun in 1812 due to the influence of Edward Jenner. In a letter dated April 1812 James says that he gave a letter to Dr. Gold (sic) on 26th January 1812. He should not be confused with Dr. Francis Gold, Otage, (hostage), who was taken prisoner on 24 May 1803 and detained at Sarrelouis and was still a prisoner there in 1813.

Verdun, 14th April, 1806

Dear Simon

I am happy to find by yours of the 10th January that you have purchased the shop &c. I wish you had bought the whole of the Property, however I am glad you have got what you have. I am sorry it is not in my power to assist you in paying for it. I am glad to hear that you and all friends are well, as I am at present, thank God. I am happy to hear that Walter keeps his health so well, he must be well seasoned now to the climate. Give my love to him when you write again. I am sorry to hear of the deaths you mention in your last. Particularly Simon Murray's. I am much surprised to find Nathan Linton and Isobel Hope married at last after putting it off so long. It is a pity they had not married at first.

We have been amused again with the hopes of an Exchange, but I am afraid it will turn out as before. If the Ministry should fail in the attempt this time, I think we may set ourselves down quietly here during the War, and which has every appearance to be of a long duration.

You were wanting to know how I come on with the French language. I am ashamed to own I have not made such progress as I ought to have done for the time I have been here. I can read it pretty well but cannot speak it so fluently as I could wish. It is rather difficult to speak it as the idiom of the language is so different from ours. I am much afraid I shall be quite master of it before we leave this country.

I don't suppose Maddy has had much opportunity of being at school since I left Langholm as Nanny cannot spare her. I should be very glad to pay half, and I dare say you will have no objections to pay the other half, to hire a girl to assist Nanny, that she may be able to get to school, as I dare say she wants it very much. If you agree to it, let it be done immediately and let her attend both reading and sewing school for a year at least.

I have never heard from Mrs. Scott, Forge, yet. I don't suppose she will write now. If any of the Richardsons should arrive in the County, you'll not forget to mention their nephew to them, if you should hear any account of the young man's father let me know. Inform me how the Manufactories goes on at Langholm, if they are going briskly or if the war has put a stop to them, and how the Woollen Manufactory goes on and who has bought it. Remember me kindly to Brother John, Nanny and the children, to all our friends at the Kerr, Crofthead, Hagg, Terrona, Carrickrig, Middlebyhill, to the Revd Messrs Martin & Jardine, Doctors Moffat & Douglas, the Goodwife, Milntown family, James Carruthers & family, Mrs Laidlaw, Mrs Moffat &

family, John Byers, &c. &c. and all enquiring friends. If you see any of Mr Bell's friends you may let them know he is very well. The Honble Mr Eardley has got leave to return to England, he left Verdun about a week ago. Let me know who has got the Post Office.

> *I remain,   Dear Simon*
> *Your affectionate Brother*
> *J. Hyslop*

The Post Office at that time was in the New Town at the corner of Elizabeth Street and Charles Street New, now renamed Thomas Telford Road. Miss Margaret Easton had been the postmistress from 1751 until her death in December 1805. The new postmaster in 1806 was William Little, brother of Dr. Andrew Little schoolmaster in Langholm, and son of John Little, merchant in Netherknock, and his wife Margaret Thomson. William died in 1820 aged 72 and his wife, Janet Pasley ran the post office. She was followed by her son-in-law John Nichol who was postmaster in 1839 when the post office moved to the High Street.

An event occurred at the end of June 1806 of which James made no mention in his next letter. His friend, John Bell, became a father and his son's birth is recorded as *Charles Guillaume Bell, enfant naturel, born 30th June 1806.* The official registration entry gives further interesting details. John is aged thirty-one, surgeon and major in the English Royal Navy, English prisoner in Verdun and lodged at Rue Mazel. He is the son of the late Joseph Bell, gentleman, and his wife Anne Mandeville. The mother of the baby is Geneviève Ancemont, aged twenty-three. At that time French girls were not allowed to marry prisoners of war but presumably she was allowed to live with him because in 1810 they have another son.

The Rue Mazel is situated not far from La Porte Chaussée. Many of the British prisoners lodged there and Rue Mazel became known amongst themselves as Bond Street, a clever play on the word bond. It is now a very busy main street.

The exchange of a few prisoners did take place in 1806 one being Captain Edward Leveson Gower who was fortunate in having Charles Fox, Foreign Secretary, as a friend. The exchange of a prisoner depended very much on his rank, whether he would be useful to the government if freed and also on having influential friends. The Courts Martial for the *Shannon* was held on board HMS *Gladiator* in Portsmouth Harbour on the 17th March 1807 and Captain Gower was exonerated.

Verdun, 28th February 1807

Dear Brother

As the communication has been shut for some time, have neither had the opportunity of writing or hearing from you. I now embrace the opportunity by a Lady who has got leave to return to England. I am happy to say I have had my health very well since I wrote you last, and would be glad to find you have all enjoyed the same.

I have not had a letter from you since the 10th January 1806. I should have been very uneasy if I had not received a letter from Mr. Corrie the 18th October last who mentioned you were then all well. My last letters to you were the 13th April & 9th August 1806 which I hope you received. Yours I suppose must have miscarried.

I would be happy to hear from you, but as there will be no other conveyance but through the Transport Board, you must write me through that channel; and if Simon Little is in London you might enclose it to him, (paying the postage) and desire him to give it in to the office, but if he is not in

London, I daresay Mr Wm Moffat or Mr. Simon Irving would think it no trouble to convey one to the office for me.

I have been obliged to write on half a sheet as the Lady has a great many letters, and have been obliged likewise to leave it open. I hope Walter was well when you heard from him last, when you write remember me to him. I have no news to write you, everything going on as usual. Give my compliments to John, Nanny, Children and all enquiring friends.

I remain Your affectionate Brother

J. Hyslop

During 1806 Napoleon decreed that throughout his Empire all letters coming from or going to England were to be destroyed. This explains why James's letter dated 9th August 1806 was lost and no further letters from home reached him for several years.

CHAPTER 9

VERDUN 1810 – 1812

The next surviving letter from James is dated April 1811 although he has sent several and gives the dates; one can only assume that they were confiscated. The situation regarding the receiving and sending of letters to and from the prisoners fluctuated considerably. In all his letters to date James is very circumspect in what he writes about the living conditions and petty restrictions so it is doubtful if the missing letters would have told us more.

The Commandant during the early years was a particularly unpleasant man. General Wirion was a promoted policeman. Numerous accounts have been written about him and it is not the purpose of this book to repeat the stories about him. Suffice to say that he was generally hated by all the prisoners. His dishonesty knew no bounds and he excelled at blackmail. He set up a secret police and had a large range of other spies. Householders were encouraged to report personal details concerning those billeted on them. It was not until early in 1810 and due to the efforts of Sir Thomas Lavie, senior British officer, that Wirion was recalled to Paris to answer charges of fraud. On April 7 1810 Wirion was found shot dead in the Bois de Boulogne; the authorities claimed that, rather than face charges, he had committed suicide.

The next piece of information about James is in a letter he wrote to the Minister of War. It is in the archives of, and is reproduced courtesy of, Service Historique de l'Armée de Terre, in the Château de Vincennes in Paris.

De Verdun,
ce 11 Janvier
1810.

N° 220.
du 18 Janvier

James Hyslop, non-combattant,
Commissaire de Vaisseaux, au
Service de Sa Majesté Britannique,
fait prisonnier le 10 Décembre 1803

À Son Excellence, Monseigneur
le Duc de Feltre, Ministre de la
Guerre. &c. &c. &c.

Monseigneur,

La longueur à laquelle,
a traîné ma détention dans ce pays, a
tellement dérangé mes affaires particu-
lières en Angleterre, que je ne puis plus
longtemps désister, de m'adresser à Votre
Excellence qui, peut seule m'accorder le
remède dont j'ai besoin.

Ce serait d'abuser des temps de
Votre Excellence, que d'entrer dans le détail
des affaires, d'un simple particulier comme
moi; c'est pourquoi, je crois, qu'il suffit
de dire, qu'elles sont d'une telle nature,
car sans ma présence réelle, on ne
peut y rien faire; car, ceux aux quels
j'en ai confié la gestion, ou ne veulent,
ou ne peuvent pas me faire passer des
nouvelles, de ce qu'ils ont fait pour moi;

de

Letter to the Minister of War

de sorte que, je ne peux tirer de l'argent, sur eux, crainte que, par leur négligence de vaquer à mes affaires, ils n'ont point d'argent à moi, entre leurs mains; ou, que sous prétexte de mon absence, ils ne refusent d'honorer mes traites; ce qui m'exposerait à des frais que je ne pourrais payer.

En conséquence, j'espère que Votre Excellence excusera ma hardiesse, quand je la xxx sollicite respectueusement de daigner vouloir bien ordonner qu'il me soit permis d'aller en Angleterre sous parole, pour un an, ou pour tel autre espace de temps que, Votre Excellence jugera à propos de m'accorder, pour arranger mes affaires; à condition de retourner en France quand il plaira à Votre Excellence de m'ordonner de le faire.

Comme je crois, qu'il n'y ait aucun reproche à faire à ma conduite; soit comme prisonnier, soit comme habitant de cette Ville, pendant le long période (plus de six ans) qu'elle a été malheureusement, par les événemens, mise à l'épreuve, j'ai quelque lieu d'espérer que Votre Excellence se fiera à mon honneur: mais, dans le cas contraire,

je

je serai prêt de donner tout autre
garant pour mon retour, qui puisse
m'être demandé; ma situation étant
telle, que je dois, sous quelques conditions,
que ce soient, accepter avec la plus
grande reconnaissance, la grace que, j'ai
osé demander dans cette pétition.

J'ai l'honneur d'être
avec le plus grand respect,

Monseigneur,
De Votre Excellence,
le très humble,
et très obéissant Serviteur

The following is a translation:-

James Hyslop, non-combatant, Ship's Purser, in the service of His British Majesty, taken prisoner 10 December 1803.
To His Excellency, His Grace the Duke of Feltre, Minister of War.

Your Grace,

The longer my detention in this country drags on, so much my practical affairs in England have been upset, that I cannot desist any longer from addressing Your Excellency, who alone can accord me the remedy which I need.

It would be misusing Your Excellency's time to enter into details of these affairs which are only personal to me. It is because I believe that it is sufficient to say that they are of such a nature that without my actual presence nothing can be done; for those whom I have entrusted the business do not want and are unable to pass on the information of what they have done for me, in that respect I am unable to extract the money from them, for fear that by their negligence in attending to my affairs, they do not have in their hands some of my money, or under the pretext of my absence, they refuse to honour my drafts; which would expose me to expenses which I would be unable to pay.

In consequence, I hope that Your Excellency will excuse my boldness, when I beg respectfully your excellency to be so good as to give me permission to go to England on parole, for a year, or for such other period of time that Your Excellency will judge appropriate, to arrange my affairs, on condition to return to France when it pleases Your Excellency to order me to do so.

As I believe that no one could ever criticise my conduct as a prisoner or as an inhabitant of this town, during the long period (more than six years) which has been, unfortunately, put to the test by the events, I have good reason to hope that your Excellency will trust my integrity; but in contrary circumstances I would be ready to give all other guarantees for my return, whatever is asked of me, my situation being such, that I must accept all the conditions imposed, with the greatest recognition of the favour which I have dared to ask in this petition.

I have the honour to be with the greatest respect, Your Grace,

Your Excellency's very humble and most obedient servant

J. Hyslop

The reply was swift and would be a great disappointment to James although possibly not unexpected.

I am indebted to Monsieur Brian Meringo who found it at Service Historique de L'Armée de Terre, Paris. He kindly supplied me with the following translation, reproduced below.

War Ministry 5th Division
Office for Prisoners of War
Draft of the letter written by the Minister to the Adjutant-Commander Courselles, commander at the Depôt at Verdun.

25th January 1810

Dear Sir

I am pleased to inform you that I have just received a petition from Mr. James Hyslop, prisoner of war at the depôt under your command, whereby he requests permission to go and spend some time in England to conclude family matters.

I request that you inform this foreigner that I cannot accept his request at this time.

~~Authorizations of this sort can only be granted by the Emperor himself and circumstances do not allow me to propose it to His Majesty.~~

Yours sincerely

It is perhaps interesting to note the text crossed out above in the original draft shows the level of permission that would have been required.

If James had been allowed to return to Britain in 1810 he would have heard that his brother John had died, as a result of an accident, on 28th July 1809 leaving his wife with six little boys to bring up. The eldest being twelve and the youngest not yet four years old. No doubt Simon would have sent the news to him but the letter failed to arrive.

Verdun, 29th April 1811

My Dear Brother

I cannot let slip the opportunity that offers by a gentleman returning to England, of writing you a few lines to inform you of my being in perfect health, thanks be to God for it; and I need not add how happy I should be to hear from you, and of you being all in good health.

I have not had the pleasure of a letter from you since 10th October 1808, since that time I have written several viz- on the 7th Nov 1808, the 14th June 1809, the 16th Feb. and the 16th Novem 1810 [none was received] *and perhaps you have been as unfortunate in not receiving them as I have. I might have remained ignorant of the death of our dear Brother, if I had not been fortunate in receiving a letter from a correspondent in Langholm, dated 29th Oct.1810, which letter I answered 14th January 1811, being the first opportunity that offered.*

Notwithstanding that all your letters have miscarried, you must continue to write me from time to time. Perhaps I may be more fortunate in future. When did you hear from Brother Walter? I hope he was well. Give my kind love to our sister and all the children. When you write Walter

remember me to him.   Remember me to all
enquiring friends.

                    I remain   Your affectionate brother
                              J. Hyslop

P.S. I am both stinted to paper & time, as I did not
know of his going till a little before.

There has been no further mention of John Bell in any of James's surviving letters but they were obviously still friends. By 1811 the restrictions on French girls marrying prisoners of war had been lifted so John and Geneviève were able at last to marry. James was one of the witnesses. In France a marriage is confirmed by a civil ceremony, which can be followed by a religious service. Their civil marriage would almost certainly have taken place in Geneviève's home village and this was followed by a church ceremony in Verdun. In the Verdun Anglican Register there is the following entry:

"At an Anglican ceremony on 22 June 1811 John
Bell Esq., Surgeon of HMS Shannon, from
Kirkoswald, Cumberland, Bachelor, married Marie
Geneviève Ancement of Verdun, Spinster, by Rev.
William Gorden. Witnessed and signed by Eleanor
READ, Alex. ALLEN of Dundalk, Ireland, Alex.
ECKFORD, RM, & J. HYSLOP of Langholm,
Dumfriesshire."

John Bell later moved to Sarrelouis to work as a surgeon. After returning to England in 1814 John, according to the Admiralty Half Pay book for April to June, is discharged from the *Shannon*. Whether John returned to work in France or whether he brought his wife to England is not known; there is no further mention of him in any of James's later letters.

Verdun, 18th April 1812

My Dear Brother
    I again embrace the opportunity of writing you by a Gentleman (Capt. Blair) who has just received his passport for England. I am happy to say that I continue to enjoy a good state of health, which is a blessing and one for which I have great reason to be thankful to Almighty God; & it would give me great pleasure to find that you all continue to enjoy the same.
    As you must have laid out a great deal of money in assisting our sister and children, I have enclosed you a small Navy Bill for Nine pounds Eleven Shillings which I hope you will receive safe, and place the same to my credit, and if there be any balance remaining (which if there is it must be very small) let it be laid out in the education of the children &c.
    The communication being so very difficult, I have drawn the Bills in Triplicate; the second and third I will send you by other conveyances and whichever of the three you receive first, negotiate it, and keep the others by you, do not pay them away. As soon as you receive this write me and acknowledge receipt of the Bill. Perhaps you may not have an opportunity of sending it to Mr. Corrie,

enclose it to the Commissioners of the Transport Board and pay the postage. Mention it in every letter you write me until you know that I have received one from you.

I hope you have received a letter from Brother Walter, since you wrote me last. I would be very happy to hear that he is in good health, when you write to him remember me kindly. I wrote you on the 26th of January by Dr. Gold [détenue Valentine Goold] which I hope you received safe, acknowledging the receipt of your letter of the 26th August 1811, as well as one from Mr. Corrie at the same time.

I regret much that I have not in my power to be of more assistance to our sister and the Children, on that account it falls very heavy upon you; but I trust that our Exchange may soon take place, & then I hope I will be enabled to be of some service to them. In the meantime you must not let them want for anything and you must keep an exact account of what you do lay out, that I may pay you my share, which I will do as soon as I am able, for the only way that we can show our love to the memory of our deceased brother is to take care of his poor widow and children and by all means pay great attention to the morals of the children, and make them keep holy the Lord's Day, and not let them run playing about the streets, but make them attend Church or Meeting House regularly.

I have just received a letter from Mr. Corrie, dated Guernsey the 19th February and am *extremely happy to find he has had letters from Langholm of a late date and that all friends are well.*

He mentions the death of the Duke of Buccleuch [Good Duke Henry, the third Duke], *Sir J. Johnstone of Westerhall and Mrs. Malcolm.* [she died in November 1811 and is buried in Ewes Kirkyard].

Let me know where Walter is settled, whether at Kingston or in the country. Write me both through the Transport Board and Mr Corrie. Give my kind love to sister and children, to Magdalen and her husband and all enquiring friends.

I remain   Your affectionate brother.

J. Hyslop.

P.S. If I should hear of your having received the first Bill of Exchange, I will not send the second and third. After I had finished my letter I found that Capt. Blair was disappointed of his passport, so I was obliged to keep it until now. It is by a Lady who
is returning to England that I send it.
Verdun 26th Inst. 1812.

Thomas Hunter Blair, an Army Captain, was billeted on the Mayor and had distinguished himself by rescuing the family of the Mayor from a fire. In gratitude the Mayor petitioned the Emperor for Blair's release which was granted by the Minister of War. However, his passport had to be issued by the Minister of Police who disliked the Minister of War and enjoyed thwarting his demands. As a result of this pettiness he procrastinated so long that Blair was a not released until the end of the war.

In the summer of 1812 Napoleon made his disastrous decision to invade Russia with an army of 600,000 men. In order to achieve this he recalled forty of his divisions from Spain. Russian tactics were to retreat and burn the countryside leaving nothing for the invaders. The two armies finally met in a decisive battle at Borodino about sixty miles west of Moscow; both sides suffered enormous casualties before the Russians again retreated. In October Napoleon entered Moscow, only to find it, too, had been burnt to a shell. With his troops starving and winter approaching his only choice was to return home. Napoleon, himself, unable to acknowledge defeat, high-tailed it back to Paris, abandoning the remnants of his shattered and demoralised army to face the severe weather conditions of ice and snow and inevitable starvation.

CHAPTER 10

VERDUN AND CAMBRAI 1813

Verdun, 7th April 1813

My Dear Brother,

Having I hope a safe opportunity, I embrace it of sending the Navy Bill for £9.11/- to our sister, which I promised and which I trust you will receive safe. I wrote you on the 28th October and 29th January both of which I hope you have received. Yours of the 28th Oct. I received a fortnight ago but that of the 29th August I am afraid is lost. When I have another safe opportunity I will send you my second of exchange, of the same tenor and date, for fear the first should miscarry, unless I hear from you to the contrary.

I am very glad to hear the good account you give of all the boys, and that they are obedient to their mother; I hope the Almighty will give them grace to continue always so, tell them I will not forget them when I return.

I send this by Mrs. Lambert, wife of our last Lieut. [John Lambert], an English Lady he married here, who is going over to England to settle the affairs of Mr. Lambert's brother who died lately. She expects to return to Verdun in six or eight weeks. She has promised to bring any letters for me, so will you write to me about a month after you receive this letter and address it to me at No. 10 John Street, Adelphi, London. I have given my Agent directions to receive my letters and send them by her. When you write always mention the date of the letters you receive but never the person's name they come by, for all the letters we send are obliged to be censored or else they would be taken from them.

Make the boys write me a few lines in your letter, that I may see if they write well and I hope they will be particular and tell me all the news, never mind how trifling, for I like to hear all that is going on about Langholm; give me leave to tell you that you are a very poor newsmonger yourself. There are many things I desired you to let me know in my former letters which I suppose you answered in your letter that was lost. Look over my letters again if you have not destroyed them and answer me these questions. In future always repeat anything I wish to know because there are many letters lost.

Let me know if the Bill I sent you last year paid what I owed you or not and how much you pay yearly to the Friendly Society. I hope you have heard from brother Walter and that he is in good health, when you write him give my love to him. Will you send me his address? If I have an opportunity I will write him. Let me know the name of the Captain and likewise the ship's name that carried him out to Jamaica. I remember in one of your letters you mentioned the Captain's very kind behaviour to Walter, both on the passage out and at Jamaica; if ever I should meet with him I would wish to pay him every attention in my power. Perhaps I may fall in with him, but I sincerely hope it may not be in this country.

I am happy to tell you, that since I began my letter the post has brought me yours of the 29th August. I find that you have anticipated my wishes in making Robert write me a few lines. I am glad to see he writes so well, and likewise his spelling; I hope you will make them pay great attention to their orthography, for bad spelling looks much worse than bad writing. You say that Robert studies Geography a good deal, I am very glad to hear it. I hope you will endeavour to get him books that he may improve himself. I wish you could get the History of England and Scotland for them to read, for it is very necessary first to read or study the history of our own country. Be very particular that no bad books fall into their hands, that may tend to corrupt their morals. If there be any particular books they want to read, and if you approve of their choice, will you buy them for them and I will pay you.

Let me know if Mrs.Moffat, Garwald, be still alive and well, [she died in 1806] and if John and William are married yet, remember me in the kindest manner to them all, and likewise to the Rev. Dr. Brown and family at the Manse.

I am very glad to hear that my worthy friend Mr. J. Byers is well, remember me to him likewise. Give my best wishes to sister & the children, to Magdalen & husband, and all our friends at the Kerr, Auchenrivock, Terrona, Uncle William Murray & family, (I have forgot the name of the place where he lives), Peggy & Mary with their husbands and all our other relations.

Remember me likewise to Mr. Robert and John Hotson and family, [Robert Hotson died 4th January 1813 but of course that news had not reached James], Mr. Walter Pasley and spouse, Dr. Moffat, Mr. James Carruthers and family, Mrs. Laidlaw, Mr. and Mrs. Brown, Milntown, Mr. and Mrs. Hardy, Castle, to the wood forester, (I have forgot his name), Mr. Armstrong, Wrae, and family and let me know what has become of his sons, Mr. George Irving & sisters, Arthur Rae and all enquiring friends. I forget whether I ever mentioned to you the death of Nesbit Ramsey's son* or not. Monsieur de Berger, his worthy friend, obtained leave of the French Government for him to return to Geneva and soon after his arrival he was seized with a fever that carried him off. I think it was some time in the beginning of 1810. I did not know of his death until a Lieut. of the Navy arrived here from Geneva about 18 months after, who informed me of it.

I remain   Your affectionate Brother
J. Hyslop

*Nesbit Ramsay was born in Langholm, son of Thomas Ramsay, 1707-94, and his wife Elspeth Boyd, 1722-95. Their gravestone is in Langholm Old Kirkyard but the stone has been badly eroded by the weather over the years. There are many gaps in the inscription as pieces of stone have just crumbled off. Nesbit is recorded as "died New Orleans, S. America, 10th January 1794 aged 38 years". On the reverse side, written almost as a postscript, is (Nesbit Ramsay was Post Regent to the General Post Office in Calcutta. Susanna his spouse died 13th July 1787 aged 29) Another person recorded is Susanna Richardson who died Geneva 16th June 1842 aged 25 years; presumably she is related in some way. I think that Nesbit's wife Susanna was probably the daughter of Gilbert Richardson. His wife, Susanna died in 1772 aged 49 after producing eleven children; Susanna's gravestone describes Gilbert Richardson as "of Langholm" but I have been unable to find any earlier records of him. He died in May 1783 but his age is not recorded.

In a thesis by Margaret Audin entitled *British Hostages in Napoleonic France* I found in a list of textile workers "Ramsay, manufacturer" and under dependants "Mrs. Ramsay, wife of Ramsay, manufacturer". It is impossible to know if this is Nesbit's son as there are no early records in Geneva.

Nesbit Ramsay's age at death has probably been misread due to erosion of the stone. If he was only 38 years he and his son would both have had to marry very young which was unusual. Men had first to establish themselves in their career and then tended to marry a young girl to ensure fertility.

During the first few months of 1813 the occupied countries of Europe witnessed the return of the defeated French army. When Napoleon invaded Russia he had an army of almost five hundred thousand but only about twenty thousand returned, all completely demoralised, starving and exhausted. Such a sight raised the first glimmer of hope of over-throwing French dominance. The Russians now steadily advanced west and Napoleon's former allies, Sweden, Prussia, Austria and Bavaria, seized the chance to rid themselves of French domination.   Somehow Napoleon managed to raise yet another army but at least half consisted of raw recruits with no battle experience.   Eventually Russia, Prussia and Austria formed an alliance and in October, after a three day battle at Leipzig, Napoleon was defeated.   The shattered French Army had to retreat across the Rhine to the original French border. Meanwhile during the latter half of 1813 the British under the command of Wellington successfully routed the French army in Spain. Wellington continued to advance and early in 1814 had crossed the Pyranees and landed on French soil

Cambrai, 24th Decem[r] 1813

My dear Brother,

Having the opportunity of writing to you, I cannot let slip the opportunity of letting you know that I am in good health, and would be glad to find that you are all enjoying the same blessing. I wrote you on the 14th Septem[r] enclosing my second Bill of Exchange, a few days after I was made happy on the receipt of yours of the 25th Inst. enclosing one from Robert & his Mother, to find you all in good health, and that Walter was also well the last letter you received from him; what a great blessing! How much reason have we to be thankful to the Almighty for all his mercies.

I was much pleased with Robert's letter to find so few grammatical errors in it and not many mistakes in the orthography. I am very glad the boys signed all their names, with their ages, John excepted. I hope in a short time he will be able to

sign his also. I hope they will all continue to be good boys; tell my sister I am much obliged to her for the few lines she sent me in Robert's letter, they gave me very much comfort indeed.

Since I wrote you last I have changed my Depot. I was appointed, by Captain Otter and the Committee at Verdun, to pay the charitable contributions to the seamen & soldiers here.

[Presumably this money is from Lloyds Patriotic Fund. Charles Otter was the Senior British Naval Officer at Verdun. He was Captain of the *Proserpine* which in February 1809 was becalmed while watching the port of Toulon. She was suddenly attacked at night by two French ships and such was the damage that she was forced to surrender.]

I am allowed percentage on a certain sum that is paid. It will be a little help in addition to my pay, it perhaps may be of more service to me if ever I should return to England

As soon as they gave me the appointment I petitioned the Minister of War for permission which was immediately granted.

As can be seen from the original text. James's letter, reproduced on the next page, was sent to the Minister of War with a covering letter from the Commanding Officer of the English Prisoners of War at Verdun, Major de Meulan. Again, I am indebted to Monsieur Brian Meringo who sent me translations of letters detailing the official correspondance.

This correspondance is shown here, chronologically, before James's letter continues.

James Hyslop, Commissaire de Vaisseau, Prisonnier anglais,
à Son Excellence Le Duc de Feltre, Ministre de la Guerre.

à Verdun le 19 .x.bre 1813

Monseigneur

Devant, par des intérêts particuliers, changer de dépôt, pour aller resider à Cambrai: il se presente, une occasion d'ameliorer mes moyens de subsistance, extremement reduits par dix ans de captivité; j'ose esperer que ma conduite à Verdun, pendant cette époque influera avec Votre Excellence, à m'accorder cette grace, dont je conserverai toujours la plus profonde reconnaissance.

J'ai l'honneur d'être,

Monseigneur,

de Votre Excellence
le très Obeissant
Serviteur

Hyslop

Letter requesting permission to go to Cambrai.

The following is a translation:-

James Hyslop, Ship's Purser, English Prisoner, to His Excellency The Duke of Feltre, Minister of War.

Verdun, 19 October 1813

Excellency,

Desiring to change depot in the particular interests of all residing at Cambrai; an occasion presents itself to improve the living conditions, extremely reduced after ten years of captivity. I venture to hope that my conduct at Verdun during this time will influence your Excellency and accord me this favour, of which, I shall always maintain the deepest gratitude.

I have the honour to be, Your Grace, Your Excellency's most obedient servant J. Hyslop

James's letter was enclosed in a supporting letter from the Commanding Officer of the Depot of Verdun, a translation of which is below:-

Excellency,

I am pleased to enclose herewith to your Excellency a request from Mr. Hyslop, ship's purser, to go and reside at Cambrai. He is a man of good conduct. He has the undertaking to look after the distribution of aid which the English send to their prisoner compatriots. I would prefer this

Englishman to any other because he is an honest man and not at all scheming and because his poverty makes it necessary for him.

Pleased to be with respect Sir
Your Excellency
Your most humble and devoted servant.

Verdun 23rd October 1813
Signed [signature unclear]

The result of these letters by James and the Commanding Officer produced a further three in response, as detailed below:-

War Ministry,
Report for the Minister, 14/11/1813,
5th Division, Office for Prisoners of War.

The Commanding Officer of the Depôt of Verdun sends to your Excellency the request from Mr. Hyslop, English ship's purser, prisoner in that town asking permission to transfer to the depôt at Cambrai.

He states that this foreigner will be responsible for the distribution of aid sent from England for the prisoners of war and declares that he is an honest man, not at all scheming and that this role can be entrusted to him rather than to anybody else.

I assume that your Lordship will see no inconvenience in allowing Mr. Hyslop to reside under supervision at the depôt at Cambrai.
[2 signatures unclear]

Draft of the letter written by the Minister to the officer commanding the Depôt of the British at Verdun, 11/11/1813

Dear Sir,

I have received the letter that you kindly sent to me to inform me that Mr. Hyslop, English ship's purser, prisoner of war at Verdun requests permission to go to Cambrai where he would be in charge of the aid sent from England to the prisoners of war.

The information that you have sent to me about this foreigner, who you describe as an honest man, not at all scheming, persuades me to allow his presence at Cambrai.

I request you to have passports given to him for his journey and to announce to the Commandant of this depôt the time of his arrival there.

To the Commanding Officer of the Cambrai Depôt.

I inform you, Sir, that I have just allowed Mr. Hyslop, ship's purser, English prisoner of war at Verdun to go to Cambrai.

This foreigner, whose conduct has been favourably noted, appears to have been given responsibility for distributing aid sent from England for the prisoners. I ask you to give orders that he should be particularly watched. The date of his arrival will be announced to you in advance.

James's letter to his brother continues:-

I left Verdun the 18th of last month and arrived here on the 24th. I passed through Sedan, a very noted place for the manufacture of Woollen Cloth, but at present there is very little done. It is a neat little fortified town, all the houses are built of a yellow stone and they look very pretty. I next arrived at Meziers, another small fortified town, it contains nothing remarkable; during my stay (which was two days waiting for a coach) I went as far as Charleville which is only about twenty minutes walk; it is the neatest little town I have seen in France. There is a large square in the centre of the town from which you can see the four gates. In the square there is a fountain pouring out water towards each gate and there are piazzas all round the square. The small streets leading into the great ones are all straight; also there are beautiful public walks out at one of the gates. It has a very large manufactory for small arms and that trade does not languish here at present.

I went by Valenciennes and remained one day; it was a little out of my way, but, never having been there, I wished to see it. It is a fine large town and has some very good buildings in it, the streets in general are narrow and not very regular built. The Place Napoleon is a pretty place to walk about in fine weather, it is all planted with rows of trees and seats placed in several places.

Some of the Shannon's people are in the Citadel. I went in & saw them, they were all very glad to see me. The little boy that I had with me on board to clean my boots and shoes &c. I was quite surprised to find a great big fellow nearly six feet. My steward was there also; he wishes much to go with me to Cambrai, so I have petitioned the Minister to permit him to come here, as I have occasion for some assistance I may as well employ him as another. It is not little trouble to pay 2,700 men every week, which is the number in this Depot at present.

Cambrai is a noted place for the manufacture of Cambrics from whence it took its name (altho' the French name for Cambric is Batiste), there is very little done in that way at present. Cambrai is a very large town, there are some very fine buildings in it. This is the birthplace of the famous Fennelon, the author of Telemachus; he was Arch-Bishop of Cambrai. I went and saw his tomb; it is only open to the public one or two days in the year. What havoc the revolution has made here amongst the churches (as well as in other parts of France)!! I am told the Cathedral was a very large fine handsome building, now it is only a heap of ruins; there was not a church left standing here, the place of worship they have now are two old Convents!! There are some very fine paintings in the one they have for the Cathedral; until you come near them you would really imagine the figures were in marble. The canal which goes from Valenciennes to Paris runs past the town about a league distance; it is carried over the river Scheldt. I went to see it, it is very curious.

I have just received a letter from Verdun, informing me that eleven surgeons of the Navy and three Officers of the Army have received their passports for England. I am very happy to hear it, I hope it is a prelude to something more general.

I am very sorry to hear of the deaths of our cousins R. Hyslop and Thomas Murray, what a melancholy fate his was, I pity his poor father and mother — a loud call to us dear Brother, "to be ready, for we know not the hour &c". Give my love to sister and the children, Magdalen and husband and all enquiring friends. Tell Robert I am much obliged to him for the news he gave me in his letter.

I remain,   Your very affectionate Brother
J. Hyslop.

After all the years at Verdun James was enjoying the freedom of his journey to Cambrai. Always interested in new places and new experiences he obviously took his time over the journey and was determined to make the most of this opportunity to explore the country and visit as many places as possible en route.

William Ansell, steward and seaman on the *Shannon*, was from Canterbury. There is no record of any acknowledgement to James's request. The reply to James's initial letter requesting permission to travel to Cambrai evidently took almost a month to reach him and a reply to his letter of 15 December would probably take as long, by which time circumstances had changed and the prisoners were being moved west and away from the French border.

James Hyslop Commissaire de Vaisseau ci devant
au Dépôt de Verdun

Cambrai
5 December
1813.

A Son Excellence le Duc de Feltre, Ministre de la
Guerre &c. &c. &c.

Monseigneur

J'ai l'honneur d'adresser à Votre
Excellence cette très humble pétition, de solliciter
Votre permission de faire venir auprès de moi, mon
Domestique William Ansell, qui est actuellement
détenu au Dépôt de Valenciennes.

Espérant que Votre Excellence, qui pour
sa bienveillance, est si éminemment distingué
en tout temps d'améliorer la situation des prisonniers
de Guerre me porte de vous prier très gracieusement
de m'accorder le faveur de cette requête.

J'ai l'honneur d'être
Monseigneur
de Votre Excellence le très humble
et très obéissant Serviteur
Hyslop

Letter regarding James's steward.

109

Translation of James's letter regarding his steward:-

Cambrai 15 December 1813

James Hyslop, Ship's Purser formerly at the Depot of Verdun.
To His Excellency the Duke of Feltre, Minister of War, etc. etc etc.,

Your Grace,

I have the honour to address to Your Excellency this humble petition to ask your permission to send for, nearby, my Steward William Ansell, who is actually detained at the Valenciennes Depot.

Hoping that Your Excellency, who for his benevolence is so eminently distinguished in all ways of improving the situation of prisoners of War, I send you a very gracious entreaty to accord me the favour of this request.

I have the honour to be, Your Grace,
Your Excellency's very humble and his
very obedient servant,
J. Hyslop

CHAPTER 11

1814 BLOIS AND LONDON

Blois, 17th February 1814

My dear Brother,
I wrote you from Cambrai about the 20th December informing you of my having quitted Verdun, since which there have amazing changes taken place, all the Depots have been moved to the interior. On the 11th January all the prisoners at Verdun received sudden orders to quit that Depot for Blois. I am told such a scene of confusion never was known, for the first division were told to march the day following and the whole were to be out of Verdun on the 13th. Those who had families were in great distress, everyone in want of money & conveyance for their baggage.

Distress is perhaps an understatement. The weather was appalling with snow storms and icy conditions on the roads. Those unable to obtain transport had to walk, carrying what possessions they could. Consequently, due to hypothermia and malnourishment, the death toll en route was high. Amongst the casualties was Eleanor Read who had been a witness along with James at the marriage of John Bell. Her husband Captain George Read and her daughter Sarah aged eight somehow managed to survive the nightmare journey to Blois.

On the 20th of January the Depot of Cambrai received similar orders, the officers were ordered to Blois & the men to Tours. I left Cambrai on the 24th

January and arrived at Blois the 31st. The orders were so sudden that the day after the orders arrived, the first division set off; it is beyond description the confusion & hurry it occasioned, almost everyone unprovided for the journey, both in respect to cash & the means of conveying their baggage. On my arrival at Blois, I found all my old acquaintances from Verdun. On my way from Cambrai I passed through Paris, where I remained four days, and had the pleasure of seeing things most curious; they are much more liberal at Paris than London, for you can see everything without costing you a farthing.

We have again received sudden orders to quit Blois, the officers are ordered to a small town called Gueret, about 50 leagues to the south of this; it is a very miserable place by all accounts. I am more fortunate for our worthy Commandant has given me my passport for Poitiers, a fine large town; the Depot at Cambrai has gone there. It is very unpleasant and very expensive to be marched about in this manner. I intended sending my Sister a Navy Bill in the Spring, but this has upset all my plans and I am afraid I shall not be able to do it — but the cause of our being harassed is all in our favour, and I hope will soon be the means of our release. We must bear it with patience.

I certainly have great reason to be thankful to the Almighty for his Goodness to me, for I am happy to say I am in good health, and not straightened in my circumstances, which is a great blessing. I set off tomorrow for Poitiers in the Diligence, where I expect to arrive about the 21st. I send this by my worthy friend Mr. Connin [Francis Connin] who was Surgeon of the Topaz (sic) when I belonged to her; he has received his passports for England and sets off on Saturday. He was taken in the Proserpine Frigate off Toulon. Remember me kindly to sister & the children, to Magdalen & husband, to Brother Walter & all enquiring friends.

I am
Your affectionate Brother J. Hyslop.

P.S. I have written this in such a hurry, that I am afraid you will not be able to read it, or rather not understand it, for I have not time to read it over to correct the mistakes. J.H.

In his next letter James, unfortunately, failed to give any account of his time in Poitiers. The war was rapidly coming to an end. On 30th March 1814 the Allies attacked Paris and on the 11th April Napoleon abdicated. At last James was free to go home; how typical of him to take the opportunity of spending a few more days in Paris en route! As usual he was determined not to miss any exciting and interesting experience.

N°.12   Horsleydown   Lane,

London.

24th May 1814

My Dear Brother,
Your letter of the 13th Ult. I duly received and I was very happy to find that you and all friends

Horsleydown Lane. Print reproduced by kind permission of owner of the copyright
Southwark Local History Library.

Horsleydown Lane is situated on the south bank of the Thames immediately down river from Tower Bridge which of course was not built for another eighty years. All the original buildings have long since been demolished, some possibly destroyed in air-raids; many of those remaining were removed during the Tower Bridge re-development and replaced with blocks of modern apartments. In the print of Horsleydown Lane the first building on the left is unnumbered and may possibly be a warehouse. The numbers then start with 1 and continue consecutively down the left side and return up the right side. Number 12 would be about where the horse and cart is shown. Later in 1846 James is living at number 41. This is the sixth house on the right, next to the house with light coloured stonework, its entrance is beyond the lamp past which two people are walking.

were in good health; but I am sorry to find that the weaving business does not agree with Robert; it is a great misfortune. By this time he ought to have been a great help to his mother and little brothers; but he must not be idle, he must turn to something else, if he gives himself up to habits of idleness now, he will never be able to leave it off. I hope the rest will continue diligent and assist their mother as much as they can. I am sorry I cannot help her at present, my expenses lately have been so great, being chased from one depot to another and then the expenses of returning home being a great deal, but I hope soon, (if the Admiralty would give me a ship) to be able to assist her. You may tell her to rest assured that as soon as I am able I will do it.

I have written to the Admiralty but have not yet received their answer. My friends here say that it is a good omen and that they are waiting to give me a ship; it is now a fortnight since I wrote, if I don't hear from them in a day or two I mean to write them again.

I had another view of Paris on my way home, I was there five days, I saw the King's entry into it, it was perhaps one of the most magnificent sights ever beheld.   [Louis XVIII entered Paris on 3rd May]   I was standing on the Pont Neuf (new bridge) when he was passing.   Madam Blanchard ascended in a balloon from the bridge, the king stopped some minutes to see her. The Dutchess of Angoulem was in the carriage with him. The next day the Russian troops (40,000) were reviewed, who defiled before the King in the highest order, who was sitting at the window with the Dutchess of Angoulem, the Emperors of Russia and Germany, the King of Prussia, the Count of Artois, Duke de Berri, Prince Constantine, the Prince Royal of Russia and I don't know how many more. I had a very good view of them all. I was within a few yards of the window. I also saw the famous General Blucher.

I was sorry I did not see the Duke of Wellington, who was there, perhaps I may see him here; the two Emperors and the King of Prussia are expected here shortly.

I should wish much to come down to Langholm but I cannot tell till I hear from the Board. Give my kind love to sister & the children, Magdalen & her husband, to all our relations, to all my friends and well-wishers (I shall not mention any of their names, *not having room for them all) but tell them I am much obliged for their kind enquiries.*

Now, my dear Brother, I must conclude and I have to beg to let me hear from you frequently as nothing will afford me more pleasure than to hear you are doing well.

I remain,

Your very affectionate brother,   J. Hyslop.

P.S. I am sorry it is so long since you heard from brother Walter, I hope he is well. I mean to write to him in a few days.

It was to be a year before James was appointed to another ship. With the war over and Napoleon despatched to the Island of Elba, the British Government, in typical fashion, was determined to reduce its expenses. Ships were decommissioned and crews disbanded.

James was certainly back in Britain by May 13th as he had received a letter from his brother Simon. According to the quarterly Half-Pay books he is being retained by the Admiralty which was fortunate for him; it was not until 1814 that Pursers became eligible for this payment. His name appears in the July to September quarter in the four shillings a day list. There were three daily rates of Half Pay for Pursers, either five shillings, four shillings or three shillings, depending on the rating of the ship on which they had served. His pay that quarter was £18.8.0d with a deduction of 4/6d, the compulsory deduction which went to the Charity for the Payment of Pensions to the Widows of Sea Officers. However there was a surprising further deduction of £1.7.3d under the heading "Property Tax". His final pay was then £16.16.3d although he did not receive payment until 11 January 1815. All such payments were at least three months, sometimes six months, overdue. Evidently on his return from France he had enough money to buy a house. Although Half-Pay was officially a retainer for officers it became, in practice, a form of pension.

As a war-time measure William Pitt had introduced Income Tax in 1799 which was abolished in 1802 after the peace of Amiens. When war broke out again in May 1803 Henry Addington, Chancellor of the Exchequer, introduced a Property Tax Bill and an Income Tax Bill which were later consolidated into one Bill. The tax was deducted at source.

CHAPTER 12

1815 – 1817

Although exiled to Elba Napoleon had many of his adherents with him including several hundred members of his Old Guard. He still had dreams of returning to France and leading his country to victory. On the night of 26th February 1815, while the Allied Commissioner was away in Italy, he and his entourage escaped and sailed for France arriving there on March 1st. By the 20th he had reached Paris and set about assembling an army although only about half of his generals remained loyal to him.

Meanwhile the Powers of Europe were meeting in Vienna. On hearing the news that Napoleon had reached Paris they promptly declared him an outlaw. They too had to assemble an army. The Duke of Wellington recommended immediate transport of an army from Britain to the Netherlands. He then set up his command in Brussels from where he could march on Paris.

Once again the Royal Navy had to prepare for war and those whose services were retained on half pay were recalled. The Warrant book records that "James Hyslop, Purser on the *Shannon* was, on April 17, appointed Purser to HMS *Orontes*". A fee of 10/9d had to be paid. The *Orontes* was a 36 gun cutter under the command of Captain N. D. Cochrane. His log during the next two months deals mainly with details of the everyday running of the ship, weather reports and the ship's position at sea. From the end of April until May 10th she was at anchor in the Downs, that area of sea north-east of Dover and south of the Goodwin Sands. Sea victualling commenced on April 16th when she took on board 94 pounds of fresh beef, 100 pounds of sugar, 76 pounds of cheese and 21 pounds of cocoa. Further entries concerning supplies continued throughout the month. In May and June *Orontes* was patrolling the English Channel between Dover and Dieppe.

Napoleon's army was finally defeated at Waterloo on the 18th June 1815. He fled back to Paris where he abdicated on June 22nd. On July 15th he surrendered to Captain Maitland on the Bellerophon. The next letter from James provides an interesting slant on the events.

Orontes in the Downs
18th July 1815

Dear Brother,

The two last times we came into the Downs I intended writing to you but was prevented both times, the ship was hardly moored when our signal was made to unmoor and proceed to sea, but to prevent my being disappointed a third time, I began my letter at sea so that I might have it ready on our arrival. I am happy to say, (may God make me truly thankful) that I have had my health extremely well since I joined the Orontes, and upon the whole as comfortable as I can expect and very agreeable and happy with all my messmates. I am also on very good terms with the Captain.

What grieves me most is the hearing of so many oaths continually and God's name so often profaned and taken in vain. I am afraid of my heart becoming callous at the frequent hearing of them repeated. I pray that the Almighty may keep me in the same frame as David was, Psalm 119 verse 136. [Rivers of waters run down mine eyes, because they keep not thy law.] *I have to request an interest in your prayers to be kept in the right way. I will be happy to hear* that you, Sister, Boys and all friends are enjoying a good state of health and that whilst we are in health we may all be preparing for death and not be putting off our repentance till a death bed, but remember the command of our Lord "be ye also ready".

Since I joined the Orontes we have been mostly cruising in the Channel off the French Coast. We lay 3 weeks at anchor off Dunkirk watching two store ships lying in the port. We received despatches by a Brig saying that War was declared with France and to detain or destroy all vessels belonging to French subjects. We just received the news in time to detain a French ship from Marseilles bound to Dunkirk, we sent her up the river, she will be a very good prize if condemned, I shall receive above £100.

On our arrival in the Downs we were immediately ordered to Dover to wait the arrival of Lord Castlereigh and to convey him to Ostend in one of the Yachts that was waiting for him. Next day his Lordship arrived; our cutter was sent on shore to carry his Lordship and suite on board the Yacht. On his leaving the shore the Fort fired a salute, and as soon as he stepped on board the Yacht we returned the salute and made sail for Ostend.

On our arrival from Ostend we were again ordered to cruise off Dieppe and St. Valery. We left the Downs on the 5th Inst., where we have been ever since endeavouring to catch Bonaparte if he should attempt to make his escape. On the 10th we were off St. Valery, it being almost calm we came to anchor. There were three boats came off to us, they had the White flag hoisted, they brought us off some newspapers. It being a Fate (sic) day with them, they invited the Captain and Officers on shore, but we declined the offer. The White flag was flying all along the French coast.

We came to anchor off Brighton and remained 24 hours, the Doctor [Robert Riddle] and I went on shore, the town was quite gay, there were a great many very genteel families there, but next month they will be much more so when they expect the Prince. We met with a Sir John Colville who paid us a great deal of attention; we invited him on Board to see the Ship but we sailed before he had an opportunity.

I mentioned Archibald Little's case to his brother but he was quite in a rage and would not let me speak, he said he had advanced too much already. The last time I wrote to Dr.Moffat I told him to give you Simon Little's address, it is No. 55, Old Broad Street. I hope the boys are all very diligent and that Simon has got his new coat long before this. I hope that James and John are also very diligent at school. How does the Park look, will there be a good crop this year? Are there many berries on the bushes? Tell Sister I will write her soon. Have you ever heard from Brother Walter yet? I hope you have before this. Remember me in *the kindest manner to Sister, the Boys, Magdalen and husband, to my friend Dr. Moffat to the Ladies at Burnfoot and all enquiring friends.*

> *I remain,*
> *Your affectionate brother,*
> *J. Hyslop.*

James continued as Purser on *Orontes*. According to Captain Cochrane's log they spent August stationed at Sheerness and then in September moved to Chatham where they remained for the next six months for repairs and general maintenance. In December HMS *Ramillies* came into harbour. Simon Little was the purser on *Ramillies* so James would almost certainly meet up with his cousin.

In February 1816 victualling the ship for the next voyage commenced and in April *Orontes* set sail once more. Her destination was St. Helena via Tenerife where they anchored on May 4th. On June 17th they arrived at St. Helena and moored off Lemon Bay and remained there until July 19th. Their next destination was the Cape of Good Hope after which they continued along the coast of South Africa. Finally, passing south of Madagascar, they reached Ile de France [Mauritius] on September 3rd and anchored off Port Louis Harbour. Ile de France had been under French rule since 1715 and was ceded to Britain in 1814.

Orontes remained at Port Louis for several weeks, taking on fresh stores, letters and packages and departed for the Cape on October 22nd. A month later on November 26th she moored at Table Bay; then off again to St. Helena arriving at James Town on December 19th for a two week stay.

On January 3rd 1817 the homeward journey began. The ship paid a brief visit to Ascension Island where they delivered forty bags of limes and collected seven seamen and three marines for passage to England. After an uneventful passage they reached Spithead and anchored on February 15th; they were then able to take on board fresh meat before continuing their voyage to Chatham. After the long sea journey the fresh meat would be a very welcome addition to their diet.

The crew was paid off at Chatham on 21st March 1817 and in the pay book James signs as purser. The ship was then decommissoned and broken up in April 1817. Once again the Admiralty was reducing the size of the Navy and many experienced men were unemployed. No doubt at the age of fifty-four James would realise that future employment in the navy was unlikely, although on leaving *Orontes* he remains on half pay and is mentioned in the June 1817 quarter. This quarter's pay was £17.19.6d which he received in December. Income and Property Tax had been abolished in 1816 so the only deduction was the payment for Widows and Orphans. In the next quarter it is confirmed that he will continue to receive a pension equal to half his previous level of pay.

Fortunately James still had his house in Horsleydown Lane so was able to settle down to enjoy his retirement. He probably had many friends and colleagues who were now either retired or facing unemployment. I doubt if he could ever have imagined what dramatic changes to his life would occur during the next few months.

CHAPTER 13

MARY

From James's next and last letter, written in 1818, we know that he is now married to someone called Mary. According to family folklore James met his future wife at a friend's house where he had been invited to dinner -------"their eyes met across the table and nature took its course"!

In 1825 his nephew John wrote to him at Gilmonby in the parish of Bowes which, at that time, was in the North Riding of Yorkshire. This letter is still extant although very fragile. John asks "what establishment you keep, if you have got a farm?".

So who was Mary and why did they move to Gilmonby? James had no connections with the area so it seemed reasonable to suspect that Mary came from that district.

At Southwark Local Studies Library I found the marriage of James Hyslop and Mary Laidman in the parish of St. John, Horsleydown, Southwark, by licence on 25th August 1817.

I then searched the parish registers of Bowes and found a Mary Laidman, baptised 11th April 1776, daughter of Jonathan Laidman and Elizabeth Bell who had married in Bowes 4th June 1775. Jonathan was baptised in 1739, son of Thomas Laidman and his wife Issabell who resided at Howloulgill in the hamlet of Gilmonby adjoining the village of Bowes. Jonathan and Elizabeth had two more daughters, Margaret in 1779 and Elizabeth in 1782.

There was no record of a baptism of an Elizabeth Bell in Bowes. As her first daughter was named Mary it seemed reasonable to think that Elizabeth's mother was also Mary. I therefore looked for a baptism of an Elizabeth Bell, daughter of a Mary, in the surrounding parishes. I found three Elizabeths, all of whom could be possible.

A Robert Bell and his wife Mary in the parish of Middleton-in-Teesdale, Co. Durham, had a daughter named Elizabeth in 1746. However this child died four years later so she was ruled out.

In the parish of Kirkoswald, Cumberland John Bell and his wife Ann had a daughter Elizabeth in 1740. There is no record of either a marriage or a burial of this child and no siblings were found. This family has vanished from the records.

In St. Andrew's parish, Penrith there is recorded "Elizabeth, basebegot daughter to -------/Mary Bell baptised 1st June 1744". It is, of course, impossible to prove that this is the correct Elizabeth but there is a certain amount of circumstantial evidence.

In St. Andrew's parish registers there are numerous entries for the name Bell. One of particular interest is a baptism on 4th December 1736 of Joseph son of Mr. Joseph Bell. Recording the father as "Mr." would suggest that he was a person with some degree of social importance. The age of this son Joseph, who died in 1794 aged 57, would fit with the Joseph Bell of Lazonby, who married Anne Mandeville, daughter of John Mandeville Vicar of Kirkoswald. They were the parents of John Bell, baptised privately on 4th October 1771, ship's surgeon, POW and friend of James Hyslop. In the Kirkoswald parish records there is the baptism of their eldest son, Joseph, on 16th February 1770 and the father is also named as "Mr.". In the Lazonby parish records of 1771 Mr. Joseph Bell was one of the Overseers of the Poor of Lazonby Division. Lazonby is about three miles south of Kirkoswald and about six miles north-east of Penrith. Other siblings were James 1772, Isabella 1774 and Barbara 1775. James died aged 18 in 1791. Barbara married John Nicholson on 14th June 1794.

In several of James's letters he refers to Mr. Bell who seems to live in London but also must have returned north from time to time if James's brother Simon was at all likely to meet him.

As James had bought his house in Southwark I wondered if perhaps Joseph Bell lived in the same area. On a subsequent visit to Southwark Local Studies Library I looked in the parish registers of St. John, Horsleydown for a marriage of Joseph Bell without success. I then looked at the next parish of St. Saviour and found a marriage on 18th April 1801 of Amey Kimber to Joseph Bell from Cumberland. Unfortunately no local address was given. St. Saviour's church became Southwark Cathedral in 1905.

Elizabeth Bell, wife of Jonathan Laidman who farmed at Howloulgill, (the spelling varies in later registers) died in December 1795. Mary was now aged 19, Margaret 16 and Elizabeth 13. They were all old enough to run the house for their father and also help on the farm. Ten years later Jonathan died and was buried in the churchyard of St. Giles, Bowes on the 3rd of January 1805. Unfortunately he died intestate. At that time his three unmarried daughters would not be allowed to take over the lease on Howloulgill although it had always been their home.

The following year on the 20th November 1806 Margaret Laidman married John Martin, farmer, in Arkengarthdale and went to live there.

There is a record in Bowes parish registers stating that Elizabeth Laidman, native of Howloulgill married Thomas Kipling, farmer and native of Mickleton prior to the 18th May 1811 on which day their second daughter was baptised. Had Thomas Kipling been employed by the Laidman girls to help with the running of the farm? One wonders why he and Elizabeth took so long to marry but by doing so he could take over the lease on Howloulgill. Kiplings continued at Howloulgill until well into the 20th Century.

It is impossible to know when Mary left Howloulgill. Perhaps after her sister Elizabeth and Thomas Kipling were married she felt it was time to look for work elsewhere. Why and when did she choose to go to London? If she was distantly related to Joseph Bell did he find work for her? I doubt if these questions will ever be answered.

CHAPTER 14

LONDON 1818

12 Horsleydown Lane, London.
21st May, 1818

Dear Brother,

I take the opportunity of writing a few lines, and am happy to say we are in good health and will be happy to hear that you are also the same. God grant that we may all be truly thankful for such a blessing. I hope Walter has had no more fits since the Dr. introduced the Seton in his neck.

You say the Boys prefer shop-keeping, they must have an education suitable, but I think if they have not left off the Latin they had better continue it until their vacancies. I should think if they understood the Latin Grammar well, they would not require to study the English much. I agree with you respecting the French language, it is very useful for a mercantile man. I did not know that Mr. Scott understood it. They must pay great attention to their writing and arithmetic and I should suppose Book-keeping would be necessary. I am glad to hear they improve so much at Drawing, I hope they will not leave it off. I should like to see some of their drawings, if there be any person coming up to Town *that you could send some. I am glad to hear they delight in reading, history is the best, let me know what books they have read. Novels are not good, they only stuff their brain with nonsense; they ought to be well acquainted with the History of their own country, Scotland & England.*

Has Sister got the Park put in order yet ? I hope she will have a good crop this year. Is there likely to be a good crop of berries? I went to Lloyd's to enquire about the Brilliant. I met with one of the underwriters whom I know, he examined the books and found she was one which he had insured and that she had arrived safe at the Cape.

I have never received any account of Brother Walter. I am much surprised that neither of Andrew Young's sons, nor John Thomson, can give you any information of him. I am afraid they do not give themselves any trouble to enquire. I think that if I had been there and they had desired me to do such a thing I would endeavour to have found him out if possible. [John Thomson and his brother James, sons of John Thomson, Innkeeper in Langholm and his wife, Janet Paterson, had both gone to work in Jamaica. John had died in Jamaica in 1804 aged 25 but his brother James was still there.]

I put on board the Caledonia, John Johnston, Master, per Leith, some Wine for you and Dr. Moffat, which I had from Sir James Little when at Tenerife in order that you might drink his health. The ship sailed last Sunday. There are three bottles for our worthy friends at the Kerr, viz. one for

Aunt Mary, one for Aunt Grizel, and one for Simon, there are three for Maddy, six for Sister and the other dozen between you and the Doctor, there being two dozen in the hamper. I hope it will arrive safe without breakage, let me know if it comes safe. I also put into the hamper the Report of the British and Foreign Bible Society, with some monthly extracts, also an old report. If you have never seen one perhaps it may be interesting to you as it will give you an idea of what is going on abroad. I also sent the Index to the Gazette &c. I was at a meeting of the B.& F. Bible Society. It was the most interesting meeting I have ever been at, there were some very famous speeches, Lord Teignmouth appears to be a most excellent man. Having a good deal of leisure I attend many of these meetings.

I desired you to let me know the reason why Mrs. Little (late Miss Maxwell) left her husband at Edinburgh, but you forgot it in your last. [She was the wife of John Little, known as Laird Little after whom Laird's Entry is named. They lived in Rosevale House.]. I have seen Mr. Waugh since I wrote you last. I gave Mr. Jardine's compliments to him and he desired to be kindly remembered to him.

You will find 10/6 in the Books to pay for the Wine Carriage. If there should be one of the bottles broken give 5 to the Dr. or should 2 be broken give Sister 5, then the next must fall on yourself, but I hope they will arrive safe. Remember me kindly to the Doctor and beg he will accept the Wine;

remember me also to the Kerr people and to all enquiring friends. Mary joins with me in best wishes to you, Sister and the boys. I remain,
Your affectionate brother,
J.Hyslop

Once again James had been recalled to sea but unfortunately he fails to mention the name of the ship. The verbal family story is that the ship's captain had specifically asked for him to be his purser. In the Half-Pay books there is a note in the April/June 1818 quarter to say that from a letter dated 10th March 1818 he is to receive full pay for the quarter. Although he does not receive this increase until a year later the increase is to be paid in three instalments and credited to the April/June, July/September and October/December quarters. It seems reasonable to deduce from this that he was employed sometime during March but was home again by May 21st the date of his letter.

Later events suggest that Mary travelled with him to Tenerife. On 2nd January 1819 their son Walter was born so he would be conceived around the middle of April 1818. Conception as late as the beginning of May would mean that a baby born on 2nd January would be five weeks premature and in those days unlikely to survive.

On the18th May 1820 their second child Elizabeth, known as Betsy, was born and both she and Walter were baptised at St. John's Church, Horsleydown on 18th June 1820.

CHAPTER 15

RETIREMENT

It has been difficult to fill in the early years of James's retirement as no further letters to his brother exist. He was no longer describing foreign lands and journeys so any letters from him would not be regarded as sufficiently interesting to be kept. However, we know that he continued to take an interest in the welfare of all his nephews.

Robert, Simon and Walter all served their apprenticeships and became masons and master builders and were able to support themselves. Robert and Walter remained in Langholm while Simon moved to Larkhall.

Of William we know nothing. I think he may have joined the Free Church in 1843 at the Disruption.

Certainly, John Hyslop, in his reminiscences, remembers that families were often divided as a result of the Disruption and admits that:-

"an aged relative of my own struck her son's name out of her Will because he left the Secession and joined the Free Kirk at the Disruption. She had seen the birth of the Secession in Langholm and with her there was no salvation beyond its borders".

This can only be his grandmother, Nanny (Hotson) Hyslop and certainly William is not mentioned in her Will. She was also the only one of his aged relatives who had more than one son.

Unfortunately the Free Church membership records cannot be found. They were returned to Langholm in 1900 when the North United Presbyterian church joined with the Free Church to become the North United Free.

In 1925 this congregation was joined by the South United Free and the name was changed to the Erskine Kirk. It continued under this name after the Union of 1929; the church building closed on the 30th October 1974; the congregation amalgamated with Langholm Old which was the original parish church.

All the church records dating back to 1781 should have moved with them but no trace of them has been found in Langholm. The Church of Scotland headquarters in George Street, Edinburgh denies all knowledge of them and, at my last enquiry, they were not in the Archives in Edinburgh. Surely someone, somewhere must know what happened to them as it is such a loss to historians for records to go astray!

The fifth child James became something of a liability to the family, demanding money from his mother and from any brother who would help him. He never settled for long at any job and drifted from one occupation to another. From verbal family history we know that his Uncle James tried to help him.

In Kent's London Directory for 1821 there is listed J. and J. Hyslop Ship's-chandlers & etc., 148, Tooley Street; this street is near London Bridge and not far from Horsleydown Lane. In 1822 they are Ships-chandlers & etc. and Stationers.

Two years later James describes his previous occupation as Grocer, which he may have used in the original sense, meaning someone who bought in bulk or traded in large quantities. The chandlery is no longer listed in 1823. After nearly two centuries it is of course impossible to prove that this actually is Uncle James and nephew, but the fact that the shop lasted for only two years certainly fits in with the reputation of James junior.

Fortunately there are further letters from James's nephew John. He served in the Indian Navy, first as Captain's Clerk and later as Purser. The letters, still extant but very fragile, cover the period 1824 to 1840. John mentioned his Uncle James in some of them and so gave a clue as to his whereabouts.

John, born in November 1805, was only four years old when his father died and was the youngest of his eleven siblings to survive; he is named in some of James's letters from France. In 1824 his mother wrote to Colonel Charles Pasley, director of military engineering at Chatham Naval Dockyard, to ask if he could provide any employment for her son.

Colonel Pasley's reply is reproduced on the next page. It is of interest to note the damage to the letter caused by the removal of the original sealing wax, envelopes were not used at this time and the letter was folded and sealed for sending. The letter is addressed to Mrs. Hyslop, Widow of the late John Hyslop, Mason, New Town, Langholm.

Chatham the 9th October 1824

Dear Mrs. Hyslop

I am happy to inform you that your son John is likely to turn out well. I intended him at first for the situation of Pursers Steward, which is a very good one, but only ranks with a servant in point of respectability. Fortunately for him, the second Clerk in the Prince Regent having broke his leg by accident, John was taken into the Office through necessity to assist in writing and keeping the Ship's Books, in which situation he gave so much satisfaction, that the Officer recommended me to try to get him appointed Captain's Clerk of some ship fitting out, when an opportunity offered.
Two days ago I recommended him to Captain Purchas of the Esk, Sloop of War, who agreed to take him on trial for a week or ten days, and if he gives satisfaction, he has promised to appoint him his Clerk.

Chatham the 9th
October 1824

Mrs Hyslop

I am happy to inform you that your son John is likely to turn out well. I intended him at first for the situation of Pursers steward, which is a very good one, but only ranks with a... warrant in point of respectability... ... for him, the ... in the ... having broke his

Letter from Colonel Charles W. Pasley.

leg by accident, John was taken
into the Office through necessity,
to assist in writing, and keeping
the Ships Books, in which
situation he gave so much
satisfaction, that the Officer
recommended me to try to
get him appointed Captain's
Clerk of some Ship fitting out,
when an opportunity offered.

Two days ago, I recommended
him to Captain Dunbar of the
New Sloop of War, who has
agreed to take him on trial

for a week or ten days, and if
he gives satisfaction, he was
promised to appoint him his
clerk. Should this appointment
take place, your son will be
very well off, as he will have
about £40 a year pay, besides
provisions, so that he may
not only maintain himself,
but save a little money, if
frugally inclined.

It has given me great
pleasure to be of service to the
grandson of Lizzie Little,
who wrote to Mine, and to the
son of John Myself and you, who
were equally kind true in my
younger days, yours sincerely
R W Pauley

137

Since I commenced this letter, your
son informs me, that he has got
the appointment of Captain Clerk
of the [...]

Mrs Taylor
Paid

Should this appointment take place your son will be very well off, as he will have about £40 a year pay besides full Provisioning, so that he may not only maintain himself, but save a little money if prudently inclined.

It gives me great pleasure to be of service to the Grandson of old Lizzie Little, my respected Nurse, and to the son of John Hyslop and you, who were equally kind to me in my younger days.

Yours sincerely,

C. W. Pasley

NB. Turn over.

Since I commenced this letter your son informs me that he has got the appointment of Captain's Clerk on the Esk.

Writing to his brother Robert from HMS Prince Regent at Chatham on the 2nd July 1824 John says "I have had my Uncle James down from London seeing me. He looks very well. He knows the Purser on board here who has interested himself greatly in my favours": so at the end of June 1824 James was still living in London.

On 14th April 1825 John writes from HMS Esk off Bathurst, Gambia River, Africa to his Uncle at Gilmonby, Near Bowes, Yorkshire. "Remember me to aunt and say I hope she is enjoying better health than when I saw her. I hope that cousin Walter and Betsy are thriving and very well and say I often think of them when walking on the deck in the silent night watch. Let me know if there is any more word from Jamaica respecting Uncle Walter's effects". Walter had died in March 1824 and was buried in Job's Hill Cemetery, Jamaica.

Mary was 43 when she gave birth to Walter and eight months later she was pregnant again. This may well have taken a toll on her health. Having been brought up in a country district she must have found it hard to live with the smoke and fog of London. If they were to move away from London then Gilmonby was an obvious choice when Mary still had her sister and family living there.

James and family were living in Gilmonby by October 1824; in November that year the Half Pay books give no address for him but his pay is sent to an agent acting for him and this continues throughout the years he resides in Gilmonby. Perhaps his visit to his nephew at Chatham had been to say goodbye. There is a land deed dated the 16th October 1824 which states that James Hyslop and Thomas Kipling are "tenants in common of a messuage (a dwelling and offices with adjoining lands) at Gilmonby and a close called Lowfield with house thereon". This is repeated again on the 1st December when they paid a fine (fee) for conveyance.

On 15th February 1825 there is an agreement between Thomas Kipling, Yeoman, of Howlowgill and James Hyslop, Grocer, late of Horsleydown in the County of Surrey but now of Gilmonby in the County of York whereby James Hyslop releases and Thomas Kipling leases "the Close or parcel of ground with a Cowhouse thereupon and known by the name of the Lowfield and containing by Estimation Three acres"

The next day, 16th February, Thomas Kipling releases and James Hyslop leases "all that Messuage or Tenement with the Garth Garden and Outhouses and Appurtenances thereto belonging situate standing lying and being in Gilmonby in the Parish of Bowes".

At the end of their first year in Gilmonby James and Mary suffered a tragedy. Their daughter, Betsy, died on 19 December 1825 at the age of five years and seven months and was buried in Bowes Churchyard on 22 December. Her burial is recorded in the parish records and the date of death is on her gravestone but the cause of death is not known. So many childhood illnesses proved fatal in those days.

Walter by this time would be almost seven years old but it has been impossible to find any local school record for him; I wondered if he had gone to Greenwich School for the children of Royal Navy officers but there is no trace of him in the school's records; no trace either in Royal Navy records. At some stage he went to sea as he is later described as Mariner so presumably he joined the Merchant Navy; there again there is no record of him obtaining either his Master's or Mate's Certificates of Competency and Service.

One wonders how James came to terms with his new life as a tenant farmer. At least all his early experiences at Old Irvine and later working on the land at Verdun would be useful. No doubt he would make the best of the situation and with his sociable nature would try to enter into the life of the village.

Very little information is to be found in the church records. I wondered if James had joined the Anglican Church and had hoped to find a list of Communicants but no list exists. Originally James was a member of the Church of Scotland but from his letters he appears to be on equally friendly terms with both the Parish minister and the minister of the Secession Kirk. While he was at Verdun he had no choice but to attend the English, that is the Anglican, church and when he finally marries it was compulsory for the marriage to be registered in his local parish. The fact that his marriage was by licence rather than by banns suggests that he was still a non-conformist. His religious fervour was normal for the times in which he lived but he seems to have been a pragmatic Christian rather than an ardent denominationalist.

Over the next fifteen years the occasional snippet of information has come to light. In 1826 James was named in the parish register as a witness at the marriage of Mark Elwood to Mary Kipling daughter of Thomas and Elizabeth Kipling. Two years later Thomas Kipling died but Elizabeth and the family continued to farm Hollowgill.

In a letter dated 20 July 1827 to his brother Robert, John mentioned that he had received a letter, while at Sierra Leone, from his Uncle James on 30 May but tantalisingly gave no further details. Another letter to his brother dated 6 October 1831 from HMS

Benares, Bombay John sent greetings to Uncles Simon and James. By now John had attained the position of Purser in the Indian Navy.

On the 6th June 1841 the Census for the Township of Gilmonby, Parish of Bowes, Barnard Castle, Enumeration District 13, Page 1, House Number 3 listed James Hyslop, aged 75, Independent, born in Scotland and Mary Hyslop aged 60, born in Yorkshire. They had one female servant.

One day in July 1841 a sad letter arrived in Langholm telling of John's death on 19th May, 1841 in Bombay at the age of 36. His death was due to a liver abscess caused by amoebic dysentery which is acquired by drinking infected water. John Hyslop, aged 13 years at the time, writing in his reminiscences said he well recalled the consternation and dismay it aroused. The letter also described the burial with full military honours. John had made his Will and bequeathed all his possessions to his mother which amounted to about £1200; at least Nanny would achieve some degree of comfort in the last decade of her life.

Some time later Walter was on a ship visiting Bombay and was able to go to the cemetery and record the details on his cousin John's gravestone. This he sent to his father for onward direction to Nanny Hyslop in Langholm. Unfortunately there is no date on this communication.

CHAPTER 16

THE FINAL YEARS

In 1844 James suffered a further tragedy when Mary, aged 68 years, died on the 31st July. The cause of death was congestive heart failure. She was buried in Bowes churchyard on the 3rd August beside her daughter. James was now almost 80 and two weeks after Mary's death he wrote his Will which is dated 13th August 1844:

Gravestone in Bowes Churchyard, photograph courtesy of Mollie Rowe, Bowes

James was now almost 80 and two weeks after Mary's death he wrote his Will which is dated 13th August 1844:

"I James Hyslop a purser in the Royal Navy and now living in Gilmonby, Parish of Bowes, County of York, and being of sound and disposing mind and memory so hereby make this last Will and Testament. First and principally I recommend my soul into the hands of Almighty God hoping for remission of all my sins through the merits of Jesus Christ my Blessed Saviour and commit my body to the Earth or Sea as it may please God. And as for such worldly estate and effects which I shall be possessed of or entitled unto at the time of my decease I give and bequeath the same unto my son Walter Hyslop all such sums of money as now is or hereafter be owed to me for my service or otherwise on Board any ship or in port, with my house, and garden Garth and Plantation situated behind the said house, and with all the household furniture. I appoint my son Walter Hyslop aforesaid sole executor of this my last Will and Testament, revoking and making void all other and prior Wills by me heretofore made and this is to be my last Will and Testament in witness whereof I have hereunto set my hand this thirteenth day of August in the year of our Lord one thousand eight hundred and forty four and in the eighth year of our Sovereign Lady Victoria by the Grace of God in the United Kingdom of Great Britain and Ireland, Glorious defender of the Faith. (Signed) James Hyslop. Signed and sealed by the said James Hyslop as and for his last will and testament in the presence of us *who have hitherunto subscribed our names as witness in the presence of the said testat. George Dent, Gilmonby, Francis Addison, Bowes, Mark Elwood, Bowes*

George Dent was the husband of Jane Laidman and Francis Addison was married to Mary Laidman so are all related to James's wife. Mark Elwood, previously mentioned was his nephew by marriage.

Locating the whereabouts of James's son Walter has been difficult. Unfortunately there are no returns for ship's crews in the 1841 Census and he is not found in the Census for Southwark or elsewhere in that region. Nothing is known about him until 1845.

The parish register for St. John, Horsleydown, Surrey records that on the 27th January 1845 James and Mary's son Walter married Margaret Nelson. No address is given on their marriage certificate but both are described as "of this parish". The marriage was by Licence which suggests that they were non-conformist. Margaret was the daughter of Peter Nelson, Mariner and Sally Mellis and her baptism is recorded on the 11th October 1815 in the parish of Stromness, Orkney.

Sally Mellis, baptised 26th January 1788 in Stromness, had married Peter Nelson on 27th September 1809 in Stromness. It may have been a shotgun marriage as their first child Eliza was baptised earlier that month on 8th September 1809. Perhaps Peter was caught when his ship returned to Orkney. Sally continued to live in Stromness and presumably Peter continued at sea but with occasional voyages to Orkney. They had another daughter, Margory, named after her maternal grandmother, baptised 19th May 1812. At some stage the family moved south to the London area. In the 1841 Census there is a Sarah Nelson aged 50 living in Thomas Street, Mile End Old Town and a Peter Nelson, pauper, Mariner, born about 1776, aged 65 living in St. George East Workhouse, London.

In 1846 James moved back to London and according to the Half Pay returns his address from March 20th is given as 41,

Horsleydown Lane. In the print of Horsleydown Lane reproduced in Chapter 11 the location of this house may be clearly seen.

James's financial circumstances had steadily improved over the years as the Half Pay rates had gradually increased. In 1842 income tax had been reintroduced by Robert Peel at seven pence in the pound but James is not affected until the tax year 1848/49; by then his Half Pay rate per day had increased to eight shillings and sixpence. In the first quarter that year his pay is £38.13.6d on which he paid £1.2.7d tax. This would give him an annual net pension of £150.3.8d on which he would be able to live very comfortably. He had to collect his money from the post office in Southwark which at that time was one of only four post offices in London.

It was not until 1848 that James became a grandfather. Mary Ann Hyslop was born to Walter and Margaret on 27th April 1848 at 1, Queen's Road, Bermondsey. Her birth was registered by her father. She was baptised 21st May 1848 at London Wall Scotch Church.

James meanwhile had moved to Ernest Place, Queen's Road. These places have vanished in the Tower Bridge re-development. He was at this address for only a short time and by the 1st April 1849 he is living at 30, Gainsford Street which is a branch road off Horsleydown Lane. Also in the year 1849 there is a record of James selling, to John Headlam, his share of open and un-enclosed lands called Gilmonby Moor.

Walter and Margaret's second child, James, was born 7th August 1849 at 54, Gainsford Street, St. John's Southwark; his birth was registered the following month by his mother so his father was presumably at sea; he was baptised on 22nd October at London Wall Scotch Church.

Sometime during the next year the family moved to live with James at number 30, Gainsford Street; here on the 10th September 1850 their baby James died. The death certificate gives the cause of death as "diarrhoea preceded by fever and accompanied by abscess of the parotid gland" so the poor child probably died of septicaemia and dehydration. Walter was evidently at sea as a neighbour registers the death. He was buried in the churchyard of St. John, Horsleydown.

Poor Margaret was once more well advanced in pregnancy and gave birth to daughter Sarah two months later on 1st November 1850; Walter was then home from sea and registered her birth on the 20th .

On 30th March 1851 the Census for the Parish of St. John, Horsleydown, Southwark lists the family as follows but Walter is evidently away to sea again:-

James Hyslop, Head, Widower, 86, Paymaster & Purser RN, born Langholm, Dumfriesshire
Margaret Hyslop, daughter-in-law, married, aged 35, born Stromness, Orkney
Mary Ann, granddaughter, aged 2, born Surrey, Gainsford St.*
Sarah, granddaughter, aged 5 months, born Surrey, Gainsford Street
Sarah Nelson, mother of Margaret Hyslop, Widow, aged 61, born Stromness, Orkney.

*Intriguingly the Census return is incorrect for the place of Mary Ann's birth.

Three years later on 21st January 1853 Mary Ann died aged 4 years and 8 months. Her father was home at the time and registered her death. Her death certificate states "Disease of the heart"as the cause of death; her burial is recorded by L.M. Humber, curate at St. John's, Horsleydown, on 25th January 1853.

To James this tragedy would bring back sad memories of the death of his own daughter Betsy. Now aged 88 and with his health deteriorating James crossed the bar for the last time on 7th April 1853. Walter was once more at sea and his death is reported by Margaret. He was buried on 15th April 1853 beside his grandchildren in the churchyard of St. John, Horsleydown.

Margaret was pregnant yet again and gave birth to Walter who was baptised on 9 October 1853 at London Wall Scotch Church.

In 1854 the burial ground at St. John's, like many others in London, was full and closed to further burials. The church, however, continued to serve the community for almost another hundred years. Unfortunately, during an air-raid on London in the early 1940's, it was badly damaged by incendiary bombs. As no one was inside the church the local fire brigade, quite understandably, was ordered to leave it to burn. Fires were raging everywhere and buildings where people might be trapped must receive top priority.

The intention was to rebuild the church but this never took place and it was closed. The actual site was sold in 1974 to the London City Mission whose building includes some of the walls of St. John's. The burial ground is now a park and is entered through the original archway. A few surviving gravestones have been relocated along one wall but most have long since disintegrated.

The park, although plagued by the constant noise of traffic, provides a welcome green space in a very busy and densely populated area. Benches have been placed along the pathways and, when I visited the site in March 2005, women with pushchairs and small children were enjoying the spring sunshine. There is a large area of grass where a few young boys were kicking a football around; certainly it is the only space available for them to play in safety. It seems a sad end to James's story but I think he was sufficiently pragmatic to have approved.

When one reviews his life James was a survivor. There was no silver spoon in his mouth when he was born into an ordinary hardworking and God fearing family. During his first thirty years he learnt how to live off the land and to battle against the elements, all of which stood him in good stead in later years. Endowed with a high intelligence he knew that his dreams could only be fulfilled by his own efforts. Apart from financial help from his Uncle Thomas Telfer, the only influential help he ever received was from Admiral

Sir Thomas Pasley. Unfortunately the Admiral died before he could render further assistance.

James appears to have been on good terms with his captains and other officers and had gained their respect; later too with his fellow prisoners of war. He suffered many set backs and disappointments yet his letters remained remarkably cheerful, but always tactful in never criticising the French authorities. He was no Pollyanna but I think he would have described his cup as half full rather than half empty. Yet he remains very human and likeable when on numerous occasions he expressed his exasperation with bureaucracy and his irritation with events.

Throughout his life his integrity, determination and innate optimism gave him an anchor which held despite the vicissitudes and tragedies that beset him. Now, through this account of his life, although buried with no memorial and forgotten as though he had never been, his name shall live.

RESEARCH REFERENCES

I have obtained information from the following list of records held by The National Archives. I acknowledge Crown copyright.

Ship's Musters

ADM36/14101	HMS *Tremendous* July/Dec.1796
ADM36/11750	HMS *Monarch* 1796
ADM36/12288	HM Sloop *Hope* 1796 to 1798
ADM36/15147	HMS *Camel* 1799
ADM36/15149	HMS *Camel* 1801
ADM36/14917	HMS *La Topaze* 1801 to 1802
ADM36/16474	HMS *La Seine* May/July 1803
ADM36/15531	HMS *Shannon* September/October 1803
ADM36/16325	HMS *Leopard* 1803
ADM37/1064	HMS *Proserpine* Sept/October 1807
ADM37/5389	HMS *Orontes* 1814 to 1815
ADM37/5780	HMS *Orontes* 1813 to 1817
ADM37/5781	HMS *Orontes* 1815 to 1817

Captain's Log

ADM51/1215	HM Sloop *Hope* 1796 to 1797
ADM51/1363	HM Sloop *Hope* 1797 to 1799
ADM51/1316	HMS *Camel* 1798 to 1800
ADM51/1359	HMS *Camel* 1800 to 1801
ADM51/1435	HMS *La Topaze* 1801 to 1802
ADM51/1378	HMS *La Seine* 1802
ADM51/2621	HMS *Orontes* 1814 to 1817

Master's Log

ADM52/3503	HMS *Tremendous* 1796
ADM52/4211	HMS *Orontes* 1816 to 17

Pay Books

ADM35/812	HM Sloop *Hope* 1798
ADM35/345	HMS *Camel*
ADM35/1925	HMS *La Topaze*

ADM1/5363 HMS *La Seine*
ADM35/1802 HMS *La Seine*
ADM35/1803 HMS *La Seine*
ADM35/3654 HMS *Orontes*

Courts Martial

ADM1/5347 HMS *Garland* December 1798
ADM1/5363 HMS *La Seine* August 1803
ADM1/5379 HMS *Shannon* March 1807

Admiralty Half Pay Books

ADM25/167 July to September 1814
ADM25/170 April to June 1815
ADM25/180 October to December 1817
ADM25/181 January to March 1818
ADM25/208 October to December 1824
ADM25/209 January to March 1825
PMG15/23 H-L 1846, 1847 and 1848
PMG15/28 D-H 1849-1852

Warrant Books

ADM6/27 James Hyslop
ADM6/191 Simon Hyslop

Miscellaneous

ADM103/468 pt 1. List of Surgeons detained as POWs up to 1st April 1813
ADM102/851 Surgeon's Succession Books. John Bell is surgeon on HMS Cumberland May 1793-November 1794.

Greenwich School records ADM73/404-406
ADM73/399
ADM73/415

BT127 Index to Registers of Certificates of Competency and Service, Masters and Mates, Home and Foreign Trade 1845-1894.

Wills proved in the Prerogative Court of Canterbury January 1853 to December 1855. Catalogue Reference:prob.11/2204. Image Reference:268. James Hyslop.

I wish to thank the following Libraries and Record Offices for their help and for their permission to quote from their sources.

National Library of Scotland
Lloyd's List 1818
Bengal Civil Servants Dodwell and Miles

The National Archives of Scotland
CH2/23335/2 Langholm Presbytery Records

Glasgow University Library
Roll of Graduates 1727-1897
Matriculation Albums 1728-1858

The Royal College of Physicians and Surgeons, Glasgow
Records of Licentiates

Carlisle Record Office
Old Parish Registers for Kirkoswald and St. Andrew's Penrith

Northallerton Record Office
Deeds, Wills & Coveyances MIC 245, Vol. 12 1819-1827

Durham Record Office
Old Parish Registers, St. Giles, Bowes and Middleton-in-Teesdale
Land Records D/HH 3/4/151 and D/HH/3/4/152

Merseyside Maritime Museum
Lloyd's List 1801 and 1802

The Society of Genealogists
British Hostages in Napoleonic France by Margaret Audin

The Guildhall Library
Kent's London Trade Directories 1790, 1793, 1798, 1802, 1805, 1814, 1816, 1821,1822 and 1823.

Southwark Local Studies Library
Old Parish Registers for St. John, Horsleydown and St. Saviour's, Southwark, Surrey,
Print of Horsleydown Lane.

The British Library
N/1/4/72 Bengal Baptisms 1789
IOR:H/67 East India Co. Home Staff appointments
IOR:0/6/21-36 Summary of careers of Bengal, Madras and Bombay Civilians 1740-1858

Church of Jesus Christ & the Latter Day Saints Library, Inverness
Old Parish Registers for Langholm, Ewes, Westerkirk, and Canonbie

BIBLIOGRAPHY

Alger, John Goldsworth, *Napoleon's British Visitors and Captives, 1801-1815*

Bryant, Sir Arthur, *The Years of Endurance 1793-1802* (1942)

Bryant, Sir Arthur, The Years of Victory 1802-1812 (1944)

Captain Hewson, *Escape from the French* (1981)

Churchill, Sir Winston S., *A History of the English Speaking Peoples, Volume III, The Age of Revolution* (1957)

The Apocrypha, *Book of Ecclesiasticus*

Fisher, H.A.L., *A History of Europe* (1936)

Gosset, W. P., *The Lost Ships of the Royal Navy 1793-1900* (Mansell, London 1986)

Hain, Sir Edward, *Prisoners of War in France from 1804 to 1814* (1914)

Hepper, David J., *British Warship Losses in the Age of Sail 1650-1859* (Jean Boudrot Publications, Sussex, 1994)

Hyslop, John & Robert, *Langholm As It Was* (1912)

Hyslop, John & Robert *Echoes from the Border Hills* (1912)

Lambert, Andrew, *War at Sea in the Age of Sail* (Cassell London, 2000)

Lewis, Michael, *A Social History of the Navy 1793-1815*

Lewis, Michael, *Napoleon and his British Captives* (1962)

McCracken, Alex. BSc., FSA(Scot) *Lieutenancy Minutes for the Subdivision of Eskdale*

Morrison, Brenda I. and McCartney, R. Bruce, *Memorial Inscriptions of Langholm Old, Staplegordon and Wauchope Churchyards*

Morrison, Brenda I and McCartney, R. Bruce *The Ewes Valley, An Historical Miscellany*

O'Byrne, W.R., *A Naval Biographical Dictionary*
Pocock, Tom, *Horatio Nelson* (1987)

Pope. Dudley *Life in Nelson's Navy* (Chatham Publishing 1981)

Rodger, N.A.M., *Naval Records for Genealogists*

Sabine, B.E.V., *A History of Income Tax* (Allen & Unwin 1966)

Uden, Grant & Cooper, Richard, *A Dictionary of British Ships and Seamen*

Wells, H.G., *The Outline of History* (1920)